SHAME ON YOU:
Big Truths From a Bad Mom

Arianna Bradford

Book Layout © 2017 BookDesignTemplates.com

Shame on You: Big Truths from a Bad Mom/ Arianna Bradford. -- 1st ed.
ISBN 978-0-578-65271-9

Dedicated to my grandmother, Ernestine, who I miss and thank every day for her unconditional support, and for my mother, Terrenna, for not trading me in for a hot dog when I was little. I love you both with all I've got.

FOREWORD

When I first met Arianna Bradford, it was at the front door of her home. We were members of the same online parenting group, and she had just had her second child a few days earlier. I, being the indescribably kind person I always have been, decided to take her a huge pan of spaghetti and bread to make weathering life with a newborn and a toddler just that much easier. She answered the door with her hair going three different ways and her eyes going five, took my spaghetti, said thank you, and shut the door. I had no idea that that brief interaction would be my introduction to one of the wittiest, kindest, and most brutally honest people I would ever have the pleasure of meeting.

We were different in many ways. She had two children, I only had one. We were raised in different environments, with different expectations. We've shouldered different burdens and lived different experiences. But, united by motherhood, we found we were similar in many ways, too. We were both moms in our late twenties. We were overwhelmed, overworked, and exhausted. We didn't know what that mystery stain was, or whether that smudge was poop or chocolate without smelling it. We couldn't find our keys, our phones, or our sanity, although we somehow never lost our knack for sarcasm. We commiserated over late nights and thrown plates, diaper blow-outs and hair tangles. We compared bite marks and bruises. We called our kids "assholes" in casual conversation, and got funny looks from the pearl clutching moms at the playground when we did.

There's something immeasurably comforting about knowing that you're not alone in the chaotic whirlwind of your parenting journey, but we live in a society that largely presents a glamorized and cleaned-up version of living that parent life. Moms are well-coifed, endlessly patient, and always well-prepared with snacks and wet wipes. Babies sleep straight out of the vaginal canal, eat all their veggies, and can recite the complete periodic table of elements by their seventh month of life. And while that may be true for some incredibly minute portion of the population, the vast majority of parents are just trying to comb what could be vomit out of their hair before they walk into an important meeting.

Things get even more complicated when we, as parents, do our best to cling desperately to some semblance of independent personhood. After giving birth to my daughter, I struggled hugely with who I was and with how parenthood had changed (or maybe just enhanced) the person I considered myself to be. I knew going into it that becoming a mom would change my world. I knew it would realign my priorities, consume my schedule, and in all likelihood, be my go-to topic of conversation at dinner parties. But I also recognized that I was a complete and self-fulfilled human being well before I ever went forth and multiplied. Learning how to balance my "before" self with my role -- and yes, my identity-- as a parent was a challenging process. Sometimes it was a guilt-ridden one. Sometimes it was unashamed and brazen. Sometimes it was joyful and easy. Sometimes the old me and the new me walked hand in hand on the beach, comfortable with each other. Sometimes the pre-kid and post-kid me engaged in all out battles with my sanity at stake. But the process was vital, because in the end, "mother" is something that I am. But it's not all I am.

While I was in the middle of figuring this all out for myself, Arianna was in the middle of a sweeping photojournalism project focused on allowing mothers to be seen as the multifaceted, complete, and complex human beings that they are. Her Not Your Average Mom project shone the spotlight on a variety of women like Arianna and myself, who'd come from a vast difference of backgrounds. United by motherhood, they approached their experiences with different strategies, using different tool kits, with varied support systems. Arianna skillfully put both their motherhood and their personhood on display, celebrating the fact that every single one of them was a complete human being outside of their abilities to raise children.

Parenting is hard, and no matter what you're doing, you're doing it wrong. That may be a harder pill for some to swallow, but for others, knowing that we're not alone in our monumental parenting missteps is the emotional equivalent of a pint of Ben and Jerry's after a rough breakup. We feel a little guilty indulging in others' tales of parenting gone wrong, but it's good for the soul to lick up every drop of parenthood solidarity.

This book is your Ben and Jerry's. It is delicious and sweet, and just like that delectable caramel core, it has the perfect pinch of saltiness. It is pages upon pages of knowing that you are not alone in this, and that you (and your kids) will be okay in the end. We are all very different. But if you're reading this book, it's because you know on some level that we are also very much the same. You also probably realize that kids are massive assholes, and you need someone to confirm it.

That, or you don't know any of this. In which case, you're about to learn.

Have fun.

-Bonnie White: Arianna's close friend, schoolteacher, and fellow "bad mom

Those Damn Kids

This morning, my day started with my three-year-old daughter screeching for help from upstairs. I had been up for about ten minutes.

I doddered around my room trying to find my glasses, so my husband got upstairs before I did. As I made my way there, I could hear that my daughter's tiny voice was filled with sadness, while my husband's just sounded like he wished he was back in bed. I was about five steps from them when I heard him yell: "Babe! I need your help in here." I sighed and enter the bathroom with full knowledge that it was gonna be one of Those Days.

The sight waiting for me consisted of my daughter standing in a puddle of her own urine; my husband standing with his hands on his hips, and my five-year-old son sitting on the toilet trying – and failing miserably—to look innocent. I didn't really need to ask what happened, but I did anyway.

"I had to pee pee and Brother sat on the toilet and wouldn't get up." My daughter said.

I glared at my son, who was surprisingly calm. He was a defendant who'd already readied his airtight and inarguable alibi. His gaze met mine without wavering. "I need to sit on the toilet for four minutes."

For the record, that is not a rule in this house. I do not time my children's bowel movements. In fact, I get concerned if they're quiet in a bathroom for longer than a minute or two. Who is teaching the boy that he must park his ass on the toilet for a certain amount of time for the bathroom visit to be legitimate?

Oh wait. No one. Because his answer was all lies. I know this because I know my son, and because I know his personality. See, he doesn't like following guidelines and rules, but he does like picking on his younger sister. And what better way to pick on someone than to sit on the toilet right when they need it, then take an inordinately long time to use it? I'm fairly certain Kid didn't even have to pee – I just think his sister's frenzy brought him joy.

I verified that this is what happened with my youngest, and then I ordered my oldest to his room, chiding him for being so mean. When I asked him later why he did it, it was clear that he hadn't thought that far into his defense. His brain short-circuited and he simply repeated what he'd said, except the rule then was that he needed to sit on the toilet for "two minutes." I'm not sure what his strategy was, lowering his own time limit on his own weird, arbitrary rule that he'd just made up, but it didn't go well for him. I do not long to clean up other people's bodily fluids first thing in the morning.

So, to recap: My kids both had to use the bathroom. My son sat his ass on the toilet first, and then he advised his sister of the new rules dictating that he had to be allowed to warm the seat for four minutes. He watched her little pee pee dance and ignored her pleas, throwing his hands up in the air like "I dunno, man, I'm just following rules." Then my daughter peed herself because she's three and forgets that we have other bathrooms in the house apparently, and she became distressed and cried for us. Then, when enforcements arrived, my son had the cojones to look me in the eyes all: "do what you must; I have already won."

This was sociopathic. This was cold. This was the exact kind of shit I'd have done when I was his age, because kids are animals. There, I said it.

And don't clutch your shirt and start shaking your head like: "Nuh uh. My Elijah-poopsie-doodle helps the poor and heals the blind and he wouldn't hurt a fly," because if your Elijah-poopsie-doodle is any younger than 12, he'd sell you out for a Tootsie Pop, and he'd probably only get upset if the Tootsie Pop wasn't the flavor he wanted. This isn't because he's broken; it's because he's a kid. And, as I have already mentioned, kids are monsters.

It's really strange that we're not allowed to say that. Parents, I mean. We all know it, and it's actually sort of funny when you think about it, but if you admit out loud that your kids are basically hairless chimpanzees, you're looked at as if you've slow-farted at dinner with a foreign dignitary.

It's almost as if people assume that our annoyance with some of their behavior means we don't love them, which is stupid, because if I didn't love my children, I'd have probably held a meeting with them ages ago.

"One of you has to go." I'd say. *"I don't care which one of you. Pack your shit and get out. In fact, both of you need to go. I've prepared a cartoonish-looking handkerchief-hobo-bindle for you and it's by the door. Live a life on the rails. I'm using your college funds to fly to the Maldives."*

I have not done that. If you're reading this book, I'm assuming you haven't either. This is, of course, because we love our kids. So we should be allowed to admit that their behavior is more than just a little erratic by societal standards. Instead, I've noticed no one ever wants to mention that they don't like something without prefacing it with "I love my kids to death, but…"

I mean…I know. I've watched them head-butt you in the groin over a juice box. You responded with a hug. You know who you do that for? People you love. I do believe that if a total stranger head-butted you in the groin on purpose, your response would be a tad more severe. So relax; we already know. You love them with all of your heart. It is not a surprise in the least.

Though, I suppose I can't speak for everyone. I've had my share of hard stares for mentioning that toddlers are anything other than sparkly little unicorns who say the darnedest things. I still remember stopping my son, at the time about two years old, from walking out of a friend's house with a candle he'd just decided he liked. I dared mention that toddlers are "the worst houseguests," to which another person at the get-together responded with a curt "It's normal. He's fine. That's what toddlers do."

Really? That's what toddlers do? You don't say, Janice. Thank you for that. I hope he steals your left shoe.

Of course stealing is what toddlers do. They also scream and kick and punch and cuddle and giggle and tell nonsensical jokes. We should talk about the first few things as much as we talk about the last few things, because otherwise we all spend inordinate amounts of time wondering whether or not our kids are normal. And whether we are normal. So y'know…talking about things and comparing notes is probably the best way to straighten that out.

If you've ever wondered whether or not you should call an old priest and a young priest on your kid, I'm here to help allay your fears. Here are some of the things that, I promise, is just kid behavior, and not a sign of your supposedly shitty parenting:

Kids are selfish (the bad kind of selfish).

I remember reading a story once in some online community or another. In it, a three-year-old stuffed his infant baby sister under the couch. The parent who was telling the story only found the baby because she started crying, and their toddler simply shrugged and said that his sister was being loud and he wanted to watch his show. Some were shocked. The parents in the comments, however, were like: "Yep. Sounds about right."

Trust me, I get the urge to wonder whether or not your kid is doomed to make it on the news in a totally not-so-good-way. I, too, have caught my children trying to shove each other down the stairs or lock one another outside. To my adult brain, this seems troublesome, and I start wondering if I've given birth to two spawns of Satan somehow (whether Satan is me or my husband in this situation, I'll leave up to you). Then I remember that they're kids, and those brains of theirs are nowhere near developed enough for them to have the empathy or the forward-thinking that we do. Sure, it seems elementary that we shouldn't roll our friends and siblings up in blankets and shut them in the laundry hamper, but that's because someone taught us that it's frowned upon.

Empathy is learned; it isn't intrinsic. You learn that real quickly when you fall down the stairs and lie on the floor below, moaning in pain while your children continue their conversation as if your near-death-by-stairs was normal. Not that I'm speaking from experience or anything. If I was, I'd also mention that they asked me when snack time was about three seconds later.

Truth is, most kids up to their teens (and further on, sometimes) are still trying to catch on to the fact that life isn't a TV show written about them, and that their behavior and their actions can actually affect real people. When they're especially little, not only do they not know this but they also don't give a shit enough to know. My son has actually started crying and screaming for me until I ran up to his room to see that nothing was, in fact, wrong. When I asked him why he forced me, a hater of all things cardio, to scale stairs for no reason, he had no real answer. All he understood in that moment was that he had the urge to cry for me, so he cried for me. It really didn't get any deeper than that.

So the next time it seems like they don't care that you're angry, remember that you're probably right – they don't. But don't take it personally: they feel that way about everyone.

Kids don't listen.

Some of you probably read the section title and wondered why I'd mention something so obvious, but I also happen to know that sometimes, on days where you've literally had to repeat yourself fourteen times for everything, you wonder if maybe it's you. Maybe, you think, the reason that your children continue to do things, even when you've specifically told them not to a million times, has more to do with you being a weenie. Maybe you suck. Maybe everyone else's kids only need to be told things once or twice, and you're just a failure as a parent. Who allowed you to watch tiny humans anyway? Someone should be fired for their shit decision-making skills.

Except no. It's not you. It's them. Most times, there's not even anything wrong with them. They just possess that heady mixture of poor impulse control and curiosity, and no one is a match for that. They love you --they do -- but they just love touching shit that doesn't belong to them even more. That's not your fault, and it's a universal thing. That doesn't make it any less annoying, but at least you know we're all in this together.

Kids are weird.

This one time, I had to leave the house for a meeting, and I left my husband in charge. When I got back, he told me that our son had gone poop, then had come to him to ask for help wiping. My husband was on a conference call, and so he couldn't help. Son disappeared. Later, husband saw suspicious puddles on the floor and shit-stained paper towels in the sink. He suspected there was more to the story, but he didn't go searching to see what that might be. Try as I might, I never found anything.

I didn't, that is, until three days later, when my son came up to me with his hand outstretched.

"Mommy," he said, his face screwed up in disgust, "I touched the poop blanket."

Ok, so, you know how you have those moments where someone says something, but it's just the right combination of words to confuse you? Like, you take much longer than you should to process what you just heard because it's weird and not something you hear every day? That was one of those moments for me. Because, while I admit that I don't purchase everything for the house, I purchase most things, and as innovative as I like to think I am, I'm certain I've never bought a poop blanket.

Long story short, I got my kid to lead me to a soft, fluffy, gray blanket that had been a housewarming gift. It was lying in the middle of the floor, and one of the corners was covered pretty liberally with shit. I was both disgusted and sort of proud that my son had the mental fortitude to use the softest thing in the house to wipe his ass. I also wondered for a brief second how this had gone unseen for three whole days, then resolved to have a talk with myself about my housekeeping skills. In the end, I couldn't even be mad; Kid had a need and was just trying to be resourceful. I mean… I hadn't ever included blankets in our toilet training curriculum, but sometimes I guess you just gotta go off-script. This was also the day before his birthday party, when we were going to have a number of people over for the first time since moving into our neighborhood. Could you imagine how that would've gone? We would've been shunned and the whole town probably would have dubbed us The Shit Blanket Family, so crisis averted, I suppose.

My point being: My son is weird and he does weird things. The same could be said for my daughter, and every kid in existence. They're like little cartoon characters with God complexes.

Sure, they do the cutesy imaginative stuff, like imaginary friends and silly stories, but I'm also referring to the things we don't know how to explain to other people, like wiping their asses with your blankets. Even though these things leave you fairly certain that you would get kicked out of get-togethers were you to ever talk about them to someone outside of your family, that weirdness is normal. There's nothing you can really do about it besides laugh and log it away for stories to tell their future prom dates.

If you catch your kid running around with underwear on his head, it's probably fine. If he starts talking to you in garbled language and then laughing, he's probably still fine. If he says the walls are dripping with blood and his teddy bear says you should leave the house while you still can, your house is probably haunted and your kid is possessed. There's nothing I can do to help you there, sorry.

For the rest of you, if you have kids who do stuff more like the first two things I mentioned, I can promise you that the chances are they're no weirder than any other kid. That goes for strange, nitpicky habits they like to enforce, or seemingly bizarre things they seem to get upset over.

That's another thing: If you're worried about whether or not it's perfectly normal for your kid to screech like you've doused their ass in cold water over the tiniest of things, even if they were happy just two seconds ago, the answer is an emphatic yes. It's an unfortunate yes, but it's a yes. I also regret to inform you that you won't see it coming; it'll just happen. And the rules will change every day. Your children are like defective Rubik's cubes; don't try to figure them out, because there is no solution. Actually, they're more like roller coasters with broken lap bars: hold on for dear life and try not to let them throw your ass off during the loop-the-loops.

And oh, the loop-the-loops. For example, did you know that the color of their plate matters? You're reading this, so you probably do. I found this out the hard way when I dared – *dared* – to give my youngest a green, plastic plate when she in fact wanted the blue one. As I placed it on the table in front of her, there was only a moment of betrayed silence, wherein she watched as I put the blue plate in front of her brother. She stared down at her own plate, and then released a wail I thought you only heard at funerals. She threw herself to the ground and actually started rolling towards our living room. She wouldn't answer my frenzied requests for an explanation, so eventually I just figured it was some sort of performance art and silently followed her. Once she stopped rolling and finally sat up, I waited another five minutes or so until she was able to speak.

"Hey there," I said with the air of someone talking to a potentially rabid animal, "what seems to be the problem?"

My daughter was doing that hiccup-y thing that kids do when they've been crying really hard for a while, and so it took me some time to decipher what she wanted. It essentially came down to that blue plate. She'd wanted it, I hadn't asked her first, and she was pissed.

Now, at the time, I was kind of dumb, and I assumed that toddlers live a life governed by facts. I tried reasoning with her. "But honey, blue or green, the food all tastes the same. Your sandwich will taste like PB&J even if the plate is pink with purple polka dots. The color doesn't matter."

She laughed at my perfectly logical response. And by "laughed," I mean she screeched in my face and threw herself back onto the floor. My son had finished his lunch by this time, and he strode over and handed his sister his blue plate. Despite the fact that the plate was still covered in crumbs and jelly, her screaming immediately abated as if nothing had happened. She was even back to smiling and telling me she loved me. I was baffled.

After some time, I realized that kids are like that person in your life – whoever they are, maybe it's you – who wants to be invited to everything, even things they have no interest in. It's all about having the chance to say yes or no. It's all about being asked.

So now, I have to ask about plate color before every meal. Sometimes, that makes things go smoothly. Sometimes, I mess up by putting a fork on the wrong side of the plate, and then we're back to the screeching. My point is, if you're thinking your kid might be "out there" because their moods are all over the place and their demands are unusual, I'm telling you they're not. They're just kids, and they feed on your confusion and pain.

Kids ask way too many damn questions.

Yes I know kids are supposed to be filled with wonderment and this is how they learn and blah blah blah blah blah, but it's really easy to say that when you're not having to answer ridiculous questions all day long without so much as a break for breath.

It's also the questions you get asked. My son will ask my husband simple shit with concrete answers, things like "where is cinnamon from?" or "How do you make French fries?" He'll ask me things that force me to get all existential and philosophical, like "What is death?" and "Why do we get old?"

We're often shamed into pretending to feel warm and fuzzy about this. Like we're supposed to paste smiles on our faces and be all "n-o-o-o-o-o, I love having to think about an age-appropriate answer to why people do bad things on top of all the other shit I have to do. I'm just so glad my children are showing interest in the world around them; this doesn't get tiring at all!"

I'm sure that some people mean that, but I struggle to understand how. Being asked big questions and small questions alike, rapid fire, for an hour straight is tiring. It does not make you want to do anything but remove yourself from the situation:

"Mommy what are bees? Where do clouds come from? Who invented robots? Why do we live in a house? Who owns the mountains? Why are you buying plane tickets? Why are you packing your luggage? What does that note say? Where are you going?"

But apparently you can't do that because it's frowned upon by "laws."

So if I have to be that person, I'll throw it out there that I hate all of the questions. I want my kids to learn, but I majored in English: I'm not the person to ask about where the color green comes from. I'm more than happy to try to answer for a while, but the human brain has only so much room for activities, and I only have so much energy available for answering cockamamie requests for knowledge. So if you've been wanting to say you're tired of it, but you're afraid to be judged, now you can just stand behind me and be like "ditto."

If you don't feel this way, good for you. I'll tell my son to mail his requests to you when my office hours are up.

Sometimes, you won't even like your kids.

I've learned that I do not quite understand toddlers.

Don't get me wrong, I love mine. I'm obsessed with them most days. I also spend an alarming amount of time stopping them from killing themselves, and it's exhausting. I didn't join a frat or a sorority in college because I didn't like babysitting mentally impaired individuals who think they can pee anywhere they please. And yet, here I am.

In fact, the more time I've spent as a parent, the more I've realized that a very large chunk of us have certain age groups that we just don't get along with very well. For most, it seems to be teenagers. For others, it's babies. For still others, it's pretty much all of it. So far, I'm pretty sure that I would be perfectly happy pretending the whole toddler stage just didn't exist.

My son was the one to show me that I am, in fact, not the perfect rock star supermodel mom that teenaged me had always imagined I'd grow up to be. He showed me this by turning two years old. If you haven't experienced a two-year-old yet, I want you to picture your sweet and happy little baby, then pretend your baby is possessed by the Devil on and off until they turn 18 — in fact, I'm still not certain that isn't what actually happens. One day, your baby will go from smiling all the time to screeching in the middle of the store because you dared to do something they didn't want. Or something they did want. Or something they didn't want and then did and then didn't again. You won't be able to win no matter what you do, and then they will ask for kisses. It's emotionally, physically, and mentally draining, but some people find it fun. I do not.

It was during a shopping trip one day, when I was clutching my son's chubby fists as he screamed as if I was murdering him, that I felt this sudden rush of resentment and dislike for the first time. Immediately, I felt like a horrible, horrible monster.

Before you ask, I get the reasoning behind tantrums, especially at that age. I get how annoying it must be to feel as if you're telling someone something clearly, only to have them look at you as if you're speaking a foreign language. I empathize, because that's me and my kids every damned day.

Take my daughter, for instance. She'll mention she is thirsty, and ask for her water bottle.

"If I give you your water bottle, don't pour water on the floor, or I'll take the bottle away." I'll say to her.

She nods.

"Do you understand?"

She nods again.

"Okay, because whenever I give you your water bottle, you pour water all over the floor and I don't want you to do that this time. You need to stay hydrated. I want to trust that you can just drink this water like a big girl. Can you do that?"

More nodding.

"Okay. So what did I say?"

"Don't pour water."

"Or…?"

"You'll take the bottle away."

"That's right. I'm going to give the water bottle to you now."

"OK."

The moment the bottle touches her little hands, my daughter turns it upside down and starts shaking water everywhere until she's surrounded by her own personal swamp. I snatch the bottle away.

"Didn't I just say not to do that?!" I ask.

"No."

This often makes me want to roll on the floor screaming, too. So yeah…it sucks when people don't listen to requests that are, in your mind, perfectly-worded. I suppose we hear about that all the time. We don't hear about how we may feel negatively towards our children when it happens though. We hear that mothers are supposed to always feel love and adoration and, at worst, patient frustration. We never hear that sometimes, we won't actually *want* to be around our kids. That happens, though, and I don't know that we should be hiding that fact as much as we do.

Like, look, should they ever want to read my words someday for some reason, I want my kids to know that I love them and that I will gladly give them any one of my organs should it be necessary. If I'm not a match, I will find them other organs. My children will never go organ-less. I never, never want them to forget that. I also just don't know if it's a good idea for them to never know that sometimes, they were dicks, and when they were dicks, I didn't like them very much.

It's not like our children will like us all the time either. Sometimes, we're going to do things that piss them off. So I don't get where this fear of returning the favor really comes from; I just know it's there for more of us than you'd ever think.

These feelings are always fleeting anyway, though sometimes they last for weeks. I didn't like my son for a couple months after he turned two, to the point where I caught myself trying to avoid spending too much time alone with him. The truth was, I was scared and overwhelmed and I didn't know how to handle him. I wasn't sure where the craziness was coming from, only that I suddenly couldn't breathe without being tantrum-ed at. Every night, though, when he'd sleep, I'd stare down at him and suddenly feel so in love with him I'd get dizzy. Dislike never meant I hated him, or that I wouldn't die for him, or that I regretted being his mother. All it meant was, when he slept I kind of wanted him to stay asleep for a while. Like maybe three days.

It took me a while to realize this, though. For the longest time, I was nervous to say anything to anyone about my feelings. I'd never once heard another woman tell me that she didn't like her kid, so I thought I was alone. A lone, mentally-ill monster. Then a friend of mine who grew comfortable with me texted me to say that her kid was being "a little asshole" and she "needed a break." She followed that by asking me if I wanted to go for drinks, then added "am I horrible? That was horrible, wasn't it?"

It was the first time I saw that I wasn't alone. That, sometimes, we feel less-than-wonderfully about our children, and that it doesn't change how crazy we are about them. The woman I'm talking about loves her kid fiercely and would probably curb-stomp anyone who hurt him. I'd never in a million years question her love for her son. But the day she messaged me, he was being an asshole, and reasonably, she didn't like him. It. Happens.

It's kind of ridiculous that this never occurs to us, when you think about it. Why wouldn't we realize that being screamed at, having to give of our emotions and our energy and our infinite fucking patience, would eventually reach an end? None of us are made solely of love and rainbows. Money doesn't grow on trees, and our emotional currency isn't born in a vacuum. At some point, we're all going to feel beat-on and tired, and it's going to ignite frustrated feelings within us because that's what humans feel when they're squeezed dry.

To drive the point home, another example from my own personal stash:

My son was pissed at me one day about something. I don't remember what it was, and I'm sure he doesn't either, but in the moment, he was angrier than I'd ever seen him.

My son is five, and he's not someone who takes very well to being ignored. I mean, I don't either, but I have to say I'm slightly confused by his insistence to be noticed whenever he does anything, even things he shouldn't want to be caught doing. Like, I get wanting my attention when you successfully stand on one foot or learn to fly a helicopter or whatever, but he wants me to notice him when he's doing shit that will ultimately get him in trouble, too. Like he'll take a pen and start drawing on our stair bannister, then see that no one saw him do it, then hunt me down and be like "Mommy, I drew on the stairs."

Then I go find it, thank him for telling me the truth, and punish him by sending him to his room. Then he cries and wails and acts surprised that I found out. I still don't quite understand. All I know is, if he keeps this up, he's going to be the worst and quickest-caught bank robber in this country's history.

Anyway.

This particular day, where he was angry at me, things escalated quickly. First, he tried screeching at me with this weird raptor screech that reminded me of my rock band days and made me laugh. Then he tried biting our couch, which was kind of annoying but easily ignored. Then he tried biting himself, which only had to happen once for him to realize that was a stupid idea. So he just started punching the couch.

"I'm not going to pay any attention to this." I said, making sure to barely look over my shoulder at him. "This isn't behavior I'm going to reward."

For someone so small, big waves of rage were rolling off this kid. He started coming closer and closer to me, alternately screeching and biting a blanket he had in his hands. Something in my gut was telling me that this was beginning to approach a line I might not want to cross, but I was too busy being responsible. I mean, right? Isn't the responsible thing to ignore bad behavior?

Who the fuck knows? Certainly not me. But I was sticking with it. I was good at it, too. I just kept drinking my coffee and browsing the internet on my phone, until my son was right next to me, stationed at my elbow. I glanced at him for a moment, and I could see that he wasn't my son anymore; he was a tiny bottle of unadulterated rage, and he wanted nothing more than to lay waste to me with his tiny fists.

I frowned at him. I made sure to give him the ultimate Mommy Face, the kind that would give any child pause. This face said, quite clearly: "Think on what you're about to do, because it won't end well for you."

Maybe the face actually said: "Haul off and punch the hell out of my arm, go ahead." Because that's exactly what he did.

He did it once. Twice. I turned to look at him. He looked at me. It was clear that he wanted to see some reaction out of me – any reaction – that would let him know he'd successfully angered me. My face stayed neutral. I was hoping that maybe he'd realize he was doing something dumb and run away. I know that if I was to smack someone with all the force I have in my body only for them to stare back at me unfazed, I'd turn tail and run my ass to a safe distance. In my son's case, my non-reaction only seemed to cause something in him to finally snap. His tiny, still-forming rational side left the building.

He hauled off and started punching the shit out of my arm over and over, as hard as he could. He was punching so hard and so frenzied that I could hear him breathing hard. It wasn't hurting me, but it was starting to stir my own rage. The natural instinct to punch back was strong; I mean, obviously I knew not to give into it, but I was really damned tempted.

I calmly picked up my phone and texted my husband: *Come get your son before I punch him in the mouth.*

Usually, my husband is slow at answering texts. I don't always know if he forgets to check his phone, or if he just reads what I send and decides it isn't worth a response. This time, he was out of the office and speeding into the kitchen within a couple seconds of receiving that message. I suppose he could read in my words that he was actually needed this time. The man gets me.

He pulled my son away (the kid was still wind milling his fists at empty air) and took him to a corner to cool down. I sat and said nothing. On the outside, I was a tree, an immovable mountain. On the inside, I was the movie *Jaws*; not the part where the shark attacks in quiet, dark waters but the part at the end where it's blown to bits by a propane tank.

My arm was throbbing a little, and my mouth was hurting from clenching my teeth. Once my son came out of the corner, I took away every privilege I could think of for the rest of the day, and sent him to his room. The anger swirled around in my stomach, and I realized that for the next few minutes at least, it was going to be a good idea for me not to see my son. I did not like him, and I wanted him far away from me. I knew it wasn't going to be that way forever, but it wasn't going to change quickly either.

There was a time when I would have beaten myself up for feeling that way, but this time, I let it ride. I let it ride because by now, I understand that no human being likes being beaten on (unless you're into that, but I'm not talking about that right now). I get that we feel like we're supposed to be kind and sweet to our children no matter what, but that isn't really a fair expectation to have for ourselves, and so I allowed myself that day to feel a little like I couldn't stand my kid's presence, just for an hour or so. After the anger and pain subsided, we went back to a normal routine, and we were back to hugs and kisses and all that good stuff. And if you think I didn't feel a little guilt along with all of that, you'd be wrong. Of course I felt guilty. I just also ignored it.

I'll get into guilt a little more later, because that deserves its own section, but for now I just want to tell you that, despite what they "neglect" to tell you, guilt isn't infallible. Feeling like a shitty mom or a shitty person doesn't mean you are — it just means you might be. And if you're feeling that guilt because you catch yourself thinking that your kid is an asshole, chances are that guilt is wrong, because they probably are being one.

I mean…Could you imagine if you dated someone who acted like this?

I can see it now: you arrive at a friend's house with this person and you introduce them. Your friend holds out their hand to shake your new partner's hand, only for your love to shriek "DO YOU HAVE FRUIT SNACKS I'M HUNGRY" as they breeze right past. You spend all of dinner telling your significant other to put your friend's shit down and to stop playing with things that aren't theirs, only to have them melt down and start crying in the middle of the kitchen. When they're not doing this, they're wandering around with their hands down their pants for absolutely no reason.

As the main course is served, your date screeches and throws it to the floor, claiming they hate broccoli. They have never tried broccoli; or, even better, they usually love broccoli. But today they do not. They didn't tell you or the host that they don't; they just decided that today, in this moment, broccoli will lead to their demise. The host moves to take it away and they screech again and demand it back. Then they scream and cry for the next ten minutes because you took away the thing they told you to take away and then wouldn't give it back.

Then as you're getting into the car on the way home, they stomp their feet and hold their breath because you didn't ask them first if they want to sit in the shotgun seat, even though they always take the shotgun seat. For the sake of getting them in the goddamned car, you apologize. Then you try to kiss them on the forehead and they kick you in the shin. Then they fart copiously on the way home and announce it and laugh every. Single. Time.

You would not date this person. You would not like this person. In fact, people would find you weird if you *did* like this person. None of those behaviors are fun ones, and call me a radical, but they don't become any more "fun" when the person doing them is a tiny version of you. It becomes easier to tolerate, because you pray they won't still be doing these things in college, but it doesn't make it any less frustrating. We're never told that it's ok to get frustrated with our kids. We're certainly never told that it's normal to not even like them sometimes. In fact, we're often pretty afraid to even say the words aloud, lest someone we know overhears and calls CPS.

We're supposed to love our kids at all times, right? Well, sure we are. As I've already mentioned, we do. There's nothing in those Motherhood Bylaws, though, about having to like them or everything they do all the time. You can love your children with every little piece of your heart and still want to put duct tape over their mouths sometimes. Believe me: they'll go through the same thing regarding their feelings for you multiple times a day. That's one of the joys of family: you get to dislike someone over and over again without worrying that they'll leave you. I guess this can also be a curse, depending on who your family is, but we're talking about your kids right now, so hopefully it's the first thing.

You are not a bad parent for feeling dislike towards your own child sometimes. You are not a bad parent for admitting that your child is an asshole, because children are assholes. Unless you're waking your kid up every morning by screaming "GOOD MORNING, ASSHOLE," you are allowed to feel as if your kid is not completely likable all the damn time. And you are allowed to vent. I can't believe I have to say these things in this day and age, but some people really don't seem to understand that it's actually tiring caring for a tiny, screaming ball of emotions all of the time.

So allow yourself to feel what you need to feel. Pretending doesn't do anything but exhaust you even further.

Kids are either big fat liars or they're brutally honest; there is no in between.

Your kids won't pick a lane when it comes to honesty until they're much older. Mine are either telling me they didn't do something when I saw them doing it just two seconds ago, or they're telling me flat out that I look pregnant, even though I haven't been pregnant in three years.

I'm actually a little jealous of them in this regard, because I'd love to be able to yell "OK, I'M TIRED AND I WANT TO GO HOME" when I'm ready to leave social events. I would also love to be able to subscribe to the belief that telling someone that I didn't do something is all it takes to get out of trouble. This isn't the case, though, and so it's a horrible inconvenience.

Comments will be made about their genitalia, the fact that you farted, and that one thing you said about your cousin when you thought you were alone. You'll never be able to live under any delusions ever again. If you find that holes were cut into all of your socks, though, nobody will know nothin'. Remember, you're a parent, so the truth only has a summer home here.

Kids will repeat EVERY goddamned thing you say, except the things you want.

You hear the jokes, and I'm here to tell you they are truth. Both my kids learned to swear by the age of two. I can't get them to learn to say "I'm sorry" or "please," but they know how to yell "fuck" in the correct context, so that's a thing.

If you can do it, try not to start swearing in front of them until you can get it through their thick skulls that they shouldn't repeat after you. If it's too late for you, that's cool. No judgment here. I'll scoot on over on the Bad Mom bench and make a spot for you.

Kids have some evil black voodoo magic that makes you forget all of this.

I inherited from my father stubborn leg hair and an ability to hold grudges like it earns me money. You would think that I'd be able to stay angry at my children for days, especially after a day where they've fought and argued – both with each other and with me -- and broken things and screamed until the air is thick with anger and resentment. It never works that way for us, though, does it?

No, you'll go to check on them at night, or they'll suddenly tell you that they love you, and it's like they've wiped your memory. All you can think about is how important they are, and how you'd die without them. You often start the next day like a goldfish that's made the rounds in its bowl: fresh and in love with all that you see and ready for the kids to start tapping on the goddamned glass all over again.

It's an evil mind trick, and you'll never escape it. It's almost as if their little instincts kick in the moment your rage reaches a certain level.

"Uh oh. She's two steps from selling me at a farmer's market." They'll think. "Time to go in for a hug and some whispered affection."

My friends with older children and teens tell me this does not change; in fact, they get even better at knowing just what to say and when to say it in order to keep you from completely losing your shit. So if you've wondered whether or not there's something wrong with you because you can't seem to stay mad, even if you should, there isn't; you're just living with little evil wizards who have learned how to tamper with your brain chemistry.

So there you have it. I suppose I could've just typed out "kids are weird. It's not just you," and left it at that, but I have a word count to reach and I'm trying to give you some extra time alone before you have to go back out there. You're welcome.

And while we're on the subject, I want to point out that not every wild, crazy, strange thing your child does will warrant an apology. Sometimes, it's just what kids do. For example, when your baby or small child screams on an airplane due to pressure or tiredness. You know how those stories that go around about parents bringing candy for the other passengers and apologizing ahead of time? It's usually all cutesy, with a little note "from" the baby, saying shit like "sometimes my ears hurt and I get fussy. Thank you for being *s-o-o-o-o-o* patient and saint-like as to let me exist within your realm of earshot, and I hope I don't ruin your rewatch of the airline's horribly chopped-up version of *Iron Man 2*."

They're bullshit. Of all of the things that your children will do that will leave you feeling guilty or worried, their behavior *as* children should never be one of them. I know we've all had moments where we've been made to feel as if an apology is in order for kids being loud, or silly, or angry, and I'm here to tell you right now it isn't. If your kid is screaming at a funeral, depending on the age, that can be a problem. If they're screaming on a playground, I don't care how annoyed Ethel is that her reading time in the park was interrupted; the playground is one of the few places where screaming and playing is encouraged, and you have absolutely no reason to worry that your children are rude or intrusive because they're doing what kids do when they play. If your baby is crying in the middle of a store because they missed naptime, it's a sucky and loud time for everyone, but there's no reason that you should have to apologize to everyone for a situation that is, frankly, a blameless one. Kids are the ultimate proof that, sometimes, shit just happens.

Some people won't get this, and they'll approach you to tell you to "get a handle" on your kid, or to give you a look that lets you know that they're irritated. In those situations, you are not wrong, your parenting is not wrong, and your child is not wrong. They are. Do not let them push you down the "I'm a shitty parent" curly slide. Your children will give you enough weird-ass behavior for you to busy yourself with. You do not need to add to the pile.

Otherwise, yes: kids are hard to deal with sometimes, and there's nothing wrong with talking about that. There's nothing wrong with admitting it aloud, and there's definitely nothing wrong with allowing yourself the grace to get fed up. If anyone ever tells you differently, send them home with your kid and don't tell them what happens when they serve up dinner on a green plate instead of a blue one.

That'll show 'em.

2

Mom Needs Boundaries, Too

I was reading some story on the internet once wherein a woman was talking about something stupid her kid had done while her back was turned. The kid was about my kid's age, and whatever The Stupid Thing was, it sounded about right. The comments she received were mostly supportive, but there were a few that really ruffled my feathers:

"Where were you? Why weren't you watching your kid?"

"Maybe if you were hanging out with your kid, this wouldn't have happened."

"Why are you leaving your x-year-old kid unattended? What did you expect to happen?"

To which the mother replied she was doing laundry or cooking or taking a shit or…y'know—something she needed to be doing. This didn't satisfy any of those people, and they only went in on her harder that she should have…honestly I don't know what they felt she should have done, because I had to stop reading so that my eyes wouldn't begin to bleed from rage.

While I feel like the attitude is starting to dissipate somewhat, there's still a pretty widespread expectation out there that parents — mothers, specifically — will fuse to their children and never ever take their eyes off their kids. EVER. A good parent, it seems, will spread super glue on their kid and stick the child to their own leg. They will shower, shit, eat, and sleep with the child by their sides at all times. Anything less, and you are a veritable trash parent.

All it takes is a quick search to see that I'm not exaggerating. Ever hear of Molly Lensing? She was the mom who, in 2016, was dragged on the internet for being so irresponsible as to set her baby down on a blanket in an airport terminal gate so that she could rest her arms during a long flight delay. Her daughter was on the floor directly in front of her. The blanket was clean and made of muslin. Molly was on her phone.

The photo went viral, because whoever the human hemorrhoid was who posted it decried her as a shitty parent. They talked about how much more interested she was in her phone than her baby. They questioned why she wasn't holding her kid. They verbally shit all over this poor woman's name and her abilities as a parent because she wasn't trying to snort her kid like a line of cocaine. The post was only removed after Molly went public and explained herself, which she shouldn't have had to do. But she did, because kids get taken away for less.

First off, Molly's delay was about 20 hours. I hold a baby for 20 *minutes* and I'm ready to put them down. Second off, Molly's baby at the time was two months old. Two month olds are barely more than sentient loaves of bread at that point, and the tricks they can do are horribly limited. How long is one supposed to want to stare at their baby before they need something — anything — else to occupy their minds? If it wasn't a phone, it would've been a magazine. Or small talk. Or tiles in the ceiling. Loving your kids doesn't mean finding them endlessly entertaining.

Third off, Molly had every right — be it after 20 hours or 20 seconds — to honor her personal boundaries. She was allowed to be tired of touching a human being. She was allowed to just be tired. And, seeing as she kept her largely-immobile child close by and in view, it really shouldn't have been anyone's concern how or when she recharged. But it was. Because people really don't seem to understand that boundary lines still exist after you have kids. In fact, those lines blur to almost non-existence to the point where you're fending off both your children, and strangers who feel comfortable weighing in with their opinions on your child-rearing abilities. Most of the time, we get so used to it that we even start to take other people's opinions into account when we shouldn't.

It's such an abrupt change, too. Before you have children, you're encouraged to enforce your personal boundaries with others. You're encouraged to take time for yourself. "No" means no. After you become a parent, though, it's like all of those things quit being relevant. If you were never a big hugger, it's suddenly a problem that you don't hug your children a ton — even if you tell them you love them and show it in other ways. If you're a person who needs time to yourself regularly, you're suddenly a monster for sitting your kids in front of an iPad or something to get a few minutes of quiet. Suddenly, we're expected to throw all of our personal needs out of the window, and it's insulting, especially when we're encouraged to teach our children about drawing their own lines in the sand. It's like everyone has to learn about taking care of themselves but parents, and it's just weird.

You shouldn't feel badly for having personal rules you abide by. And I get it: there are some you just can't enforce. I'd really love to shower without leaving the door open, for example. Call me weird, but it feels really strange looking through the glass doors to see my son staring up at me expectantly. I mean, I know he's not thinking of the fact that I'm naked so much as the fact that he wants a snack, but I kind of miss being naked without an audience. Thing is, I know that I can't close my bathroom door all the way, because that's how we wind up with broken furniture or sinks overflowing. So yeah, I get that there are just some fences we can't put up.

But dammit, there are some things we just don't have to do. Like listen all day every day to kids' music, for example. Who started this lie? Who went out there and said that you're a terrible parent if you don't listen to Wheels on The Bus 4,000 times in a row on demand for your kid? I'd love to meet that person and trip them into traffic. You think the sound of them getting hit by the grille on the bus would be *thump thump thump* or *whack whack whack*?

Anyway.

While some would disagree with me on this, I've started setting personal boundaries with my kids when I can, because there are things I just don't do. For example, horseplay. I don't wrestle or flip or flop or any of those other things because I have the physical strength of a half-dead animal and I often get hurt. My children used to try to make me do this anyway, and I used to feel like I had to let them. After getting kicked in the nose and having my ear bruised, I finally decided to say something.

"Hey," I said, "I don't like that. Please stop."

My kids continued, because as mentioned before, kids don't give a shit about your pitiful pleas for mercy.

"HEY." I said, more forcefully this time. "When someone says to stop, you stop. I don't like playing this way, and if you keep it up I'm leaving the room. Do I make myself clear?"

Wouldn't you know it? The kids actually stopped hopping on me. They were shocked that I didn't want to do something they wanted to do, and so was the Guilt Monster living in my brain. As we all know, moms have giant Guilt Monsters who tell us that literally everything we do is abuse, and that we're ruining our children for life. My Guilt Monster in that moment was hissing at me in a voice that sounded eerily like Willem Dafoe's.

"Arianna, they're only small for so long." It said. "You're stopping them from having fun. This is a thing that children do."

And for a moment, I almost wavered. Then I remembered that eating boogers and licking walls are also "things that children do," and I shook myself and stood firm. There are plenty of other little things I can do with my children that I enjoy, too, and I'm allowed to not want to do something that makes me uncomfortable. Parenthood is fraught with discomfort that we have to put up with every day, so I think we're good to deny a few bits of it here and there.

I realized this after my daughter woke up on the wrong side of the bed one morning. She was upset that she had to exist, and had decided to take it out on me. She screamed at me, tried to hit me, and told me she didn't like me from the moment she opened her eyes. At first, I tried to be understanding because I feel like doing that to the general public most days, but after a while, I began to feel hurt. You never think that someone so tiny can hurt your feelings in such a big way, but there's something about the absolution of it that really chips away at your resolve. Like, an adult can be mean, but there always seems to be a small bit of reason or vulnerability to it. Kids will lash out at you with pure hatred and anger that just is, with nothing to soften it. When you love them as much as you do, that starts to affect you, even if you rationally know you've done nothing to deserve it.

So that particular day, after finally telling her to go sit away from me for a bit, she came to me and asked for a hug. Despite what all the mommy books out there seem to say, I told her no. I mean...I didn't just tell her "no." I explained why. I told her that she'd been mean all day and that my feelings were hurt, and that I didn't feel like hugging her right then. But the gist of all of that was that I told her no. And she accepted it. What else was she going to do? Chase after me and force me? I can climb on a counter or something and she can't. She knew she was bested.

In all seriousness, not only did she accept my personal boundary, she seemed to understand it. Later, when things had calmed down a little, I did hug her as she'd requested, to which she responded by initially hugging me back and then telling me to get off of her.

I thought about this later, and I realized that I'm ok with what I did, even if some people think it's heartless. Someone has to teach our kids that parents are human, too; might as well be us...y'know, the actual parents themselves. It's important that we get through to them nice and early that jerk behavior may lead to people not wanting to be around them, and it's probably best for them to learn this from someone who won't teach them this by punching them in the jaw. If that doesn't do it for you, look at it this way: someday, they might become parents, too. Do you want them feeling like they can't have emotions or boundaries or thoughts of their own, like many of us do? Probably not. So I think it's OK.

And another thing: Just as our children are allowed to deny affection when they don't want to give it, we're allowed to do the same. I'm not talking about withholding love as a tool or punishing children by refusing to give them hugs. I mean if your kid has been crawling all over you for the last hour and then wants you to hug them over and over and over again, it's totally understandable to say "Hey, I'm all touched out. I'll give you a hug later. Please just let me sit here." Anyone who says otherwise concerns me.

Here's why: the main argument I seem to hear when I bring up a mother's bodily autonomy is "well you don't have much longer before they won't want hugs from you."

I don't know how to transcribe a fart noise, so make one with your mouth, because that's how I feel about that excuse.

This and "enjoy every moment" are platitudes that do absolutely nothing but piss off parents who are already balancing their own guilt with a need for a little goddamned autonomy. They're only said when things are particularly difficult, or when we reach our breaking points, and they only serve to belittle our frustrations and inject us with even more unnecessary guilt. It's literally impossible to enjoy everything about a person who demands with impunity that you wipe them immediately after they've monstrously shat. As mentioned before, you are going to need space sometimes. And trying to squeeze everything out of every moment of life will drive you, and everyone around you, off the deep end.

A moment had out of fear of loss is not a genuine moment. If I'm merely holding my child because someday they won't want me to anymore, I'm not doing it because I want to cuddle them or hug them close or listen to the music of their tiny giggles. Instead, I'd be doing it because I feel guilty. That's not the way love should be given, and I'm not going to set them up to learn that it is. Besides, that's a lot to put on yourself, to fear that you're not making the most of every possible moment at any given time. Do you know how many moments life is made of? I'm not so good at the maths, but I'm pretty sure it's a very high number.

Don't get me wrong – I want people to parent how they see fit, within reason. You want to hug your child every time they cry for it, I say go for it. But don't look your nose down at those who don't re-center or recharge with human touch, and don't expect those people – because that's what they still are even after having children: people – to erase that part of themselves in order to become the parents that television tells us they should be.

Short and short of it? Children own our time, our patience, and half of our blankets for some reason. They don't own our bodies, not all the way anyway. We shouldn't be made to feel guilty for recognizing this fact. The idea that parents' boundaries disappear completely is an outdated one, and it's not worth entertaining. Living purely for your kids with absolutely no walls put up for yourself is asking for disaster. Do you want to raise Norman Bates? Because that's how you raise Norman Bates.

Allow yourself to be you just a little. You'd be surprised how much closer you feel to others when you're allowed to hold on to a bit more of yourself.

All of this being said...

Sometimes, pushing your boundaries is necessary. Clearly, I'm all about telling kids not to touch your shit, and I'm all about telling other adults when it's time to go. Like, houseguests that show up at 1 PM and then are still at my house by 9PM are going to be advised of my boundaries when I stand up, disappear to my bedroom, and turn off the lights. I may open the front door before I do that, though, to help them find their way out. I'm not a total asshole.

Where was I? Oh yeah.

Obviously I think that every adult — whether they have kids or not — has the right to honor their personal boundaries. That's what this whole chapter was about. I also think, though, that sometimes our own lines have to be crossed. It can be to help our kids, or to help ourselves, but sometimes we will find that our own personal rules need a good challenging. Sometimes, it's going to be pushed upon us, and we're going to have no choice but to put up or shut up. That's not just parenting, my friends. That's life, and that can be totally okay.

Of course, I have an example of my own, and it's even a time I pushed myself *for* myself. It takes place in February of 2018, when my husband and I went to Costa Rica. It was horrible.

Not the country, mind you. Costa Rica itself was unbelievably beautiful. In fact, it was so beautiful that I would have moments where I'd forget for a second how miserable I was because the sunshine would be so warm. Or I'd actually feel a little less of a flipping in my belly because my ears would catch the soothing hiss of wind blowing through palm tree leaves. People were smiling all around and offering us free alcohol and coffee at every turn, and every single person at the resort seemed legitimately happy to help us. I can't say enough that I loved the country.

No, Costa Rica was horrible because of the constant barrage of bad news that hit us from back home, and I will get into that crazy saga later. For now, though, I want to talk about one day during that trip in particular.

It was our third day in the country, and an excursion day. My husband and I had signed up for an eco-park. I'd never heard of one before, but I was really impressed with how many things there were to do. There was a natural water slide, fresh Costa Rican coffee, horseback riding, and a hot spring. It was really a day meant to take hours of your energy, and at 32 I felt a little too old for this mess. But I loved it anyway.

Well, I loved all but the zip lining. Before we get into that, you have to understand that I am terrified of heights. I'm not so bad that I can't walk on a roof or on a ladder, but I have a problem with heights that would certainly kill me were I to fall from them, like skyscrapers, or mountains.

Or canyons. Which we just so happened to be zip lining above.

During the walk up, I kept trying to tell myself that my fear wasn't that serious. I kept trying to lie to myself and say that all I had to do was force myself to go, and I'd do it. I'd do it, and I'd be so proud of myself for overcoming a horrible fear, and I'd be able to drink in celebration that night. I'd be an inspiration to all.

As the nice supervising gentleman told us how zip lining worked, I nodded along with everyone else, as if a separate voice wasn't in the back of my head screeching "OH MY GOD WE'RE GOING TO DIE! HAVEN'T YOU WATCHED ENOUGH MOVIES??" I smiled at the people around me and made jokes about my fear, like it was just a little thing instead of a monster fearfully trying to scratch its way out of my stomach through my belly button.

The closer I got to the top, the more I could feel tears welling up in my eyes. We were hundreds of feet up and still going, and some of my built-up bravery seemed to leave, piece-by-piece, with each person who shoved off from the landing at the top. I eventually got far enough up the stairs to see where they were going, and the line went over a huge chasm. I got to the landing we were supposed to launch from, and I looked down. We were so far up that I couldn't see the jungle floor at all. Wind whistled past my ears. Somewhere in the distance, a crow cawed.

Fuck this.

I turned and started making my way down. In that moment, I didn't care if anyone was laughing. I didn't care that I wasn't going to be defeating my fears. Who said I didn't like my fears? They'd kept me alive this long, hadn't they? You know what I hadn't done in all my years of life? Died. Died by falling from something high. I wasn't doing this.

Our guide suddenly stepped in front of me. "Where are you going?"

I answered that I was heading down the stairs because I was scared of heights.

Our guide regarded me for a split second before nodding. "Would you go with someone else? If someone went with you?"

I stared, trying to imagine how one would zip line with someone else. Finally: "Sure, I guess."

As soon as I answered, the guide said something into a walkie-talkie, and like magic another, stouter man appeared. He had a friendly enough face, but it was clear they called him for things like this often, and his eyes said that he was probably going to laugh about me later. The two men chattered with each other in Spanish for a minute before he held out his hand and said "Call me Nacho."

I waved at Nacho and shakily followed him up to the platform. With the air of someone who was fixing himself the same bowl of cereal he did every morning, Nacho hopped up and hooked himself to the zip line, then motioned for me to do the same. With a little help, I did so. He then motioned from me to himself. "Wrap your legs."

I stopped staring below us to look at him with confusion. He motioned again, and I got that he was telling me to wrap my legs around him. Hesitantly, I obliged. He immediately pushed off.

I didn't scream in his ear. I'm proud of that. On the other hand, I didn't scream because I was petrified and I was making every effort to stare straight ahead the whole time. You take your wins where you can get them, I guess.

It went like that for the rest of the course, me floating, horrified, above Costa Rican jungle with my legs wrapped around a stout dude named Nacho. Just like Nature intended. Despite the terror in my heart, something interesting happened about halfway through. My heart rate slowed, and I caught myself looking around as we went. On one line, my eyes followed a winding river that was running below us. On another, I watched as a bird soared above a few of the trees below us. I felt shock at the jungle around us, and amazement at all of the green we shot through like Tarzan on his vine. It was the most beautiful thing I'd ever seen. At one point, I even felt a little excited at the sound of the wind in my ears as we rode. I can't say when this occurred, but in that moment, it became a really cool tour of the air rather than a horrifying nightmare. I felt like I'd made it over a hump, and a little swell of pride resided in my stomach where my fear once had.

We came to the last platform. It was lower than all the others, only a few feet off the ground. Nacho detached himself from our line and turned to me. "You have fun?" He asked. I nodded. He seemed genuinely happy about that.

He motioned to the tiny line ahead of us, one that wasn't high off of the ground at all, just barely too high to jump from to the ground. "Want to try that one by yourself?"

Hell no, I didn't go by myself. You bet your ass I still wrapped my legs around that man and made him take me down to solid earth. Baby steps.

My point here is that we can totally hold our ground when we need to, but there will be times where we suddenly have to make allowances. In all phases of life, those are just as common as when it makes sense to stick to your guns. Especially after we have children, when it's generally frowned upon to throw your newborn at a spider simply because you have arachnophobia. If you want peace and stability, both at home and within yourself, you're going to have to be willing to test your limits once in a while. Just don't let others dictate when and how much you'll be tested.

Allow yourself to know your own restrictions, and don't be afraid to stick to them. If you have to go beyond them, remember that you're still in charge of how far you'll go. Push a little, or push a lot. Whatever you decide to do, there's beautiful stuff to see regardless.

3

You Think You Know, But You Have No Idea

Admittedly, if someone was to try to write a book talking about all the screwy things parenthood visits upon us, it would be volumes long, and then it still wouldn't even be complete. It's kind of a joke, really: like, there are universal things that most people may go through, but there's really no constant besides a baby. You have lucky women who don't experience contractions during birth, children who are probably pod-people who never talk back, and people who actually enjoy the potty training process. There's no one way to parent, there's no one parenting experience, and it's both cool and frustrating.

So when I talk about these things that I wish someone had put in a parenting manual somewhere, these are really my own personal complaints. Some of you out there will relate, which is the point, but I know some of you will be all "that's not me. You suck, Arianna. Thumbs down." Either is fine. I just really need someone with more expertise in child-rearing to hear me out and get to work on books about these things. I also ask that I be in the acknowledgments somewhere because this was my idea. Please and thank you.

Body Problems

You know what I wish someone had told me? That you'd basically have to go through the five stages of grief for your pre-kid body, because it's gonna change on you in ways you never even anticipated.

First, you'll go through denial, where you're telling yourself that the whole thing is just temporary. Sure, your back hurts all the time now and your boobs are starting to remind you of balloons with all the air let out of them, but it'll all come back, right? Our bodies are resilient and we're just going to snap back like rubber bands right? Right.

Except no, so then we move on to anger, where we start blaming stupid pants for being restricting and we blame shirts for getting tighter, and we blame the universe for making the guy who made bathroom scales. You know that guy's name is Richard Salter? You start wishing you could find Richard Salter so that you could punch him in his throat. He ruined your life. Fuck that guy.

After that, we skate right into bargaining, where we start watching our diet a little. We say we'll only eat salads and smoothies Monday through Friday if we're allowed to bathe in tubs of nacho cheese on Saturdays and Sundays. We promise the powers that be that if we can just find clothes that will hide the stretch marks in our next family photo, we'll donate our lives to charity. We even still sprinkle a little denial in there, pretending that everything in our body still works exactly the same way, and the only problem is how we're looking on the outside.

We never do find those clothes we were looking for, and so this, plus a host of other shit, puts us in the throes of depression. We're seconds away from wearing potato sacks instead, and we kind of want to yell "YOU DID THIS TO ME!" at our children and spouse twice a day. Sadly, some of us don't get out of this stage, and it's incredibly hard to do without a nice, strong support system to help us figure out our options. Check on your friends, folks, it's not always obvious.

Finally, we reach acceptance. We realize that we can work out, but that may not get rid of our scars. Our veins or darkened skin or lost hair stops bothering us every time we look in the mirror, and it kind of just becomes a thing we might fix someday, but maybe not because that money could also go to other things. We become mostly cool with our bodies, and we come to understand that it's just life now, like pooping with an audience, or eating leftover chicken nuggets for dinner.

I can hear the weight loss gurus and personal trainers out there frothing at the mouth about this. I feel like I'm constantly hearing that because some crazy-fit mom in Hoboken ran a marathon as she birthed her baby, it means every single one of us could do the exact same thing if we just wanted it hard enough.

"The baby was still on its umbilical cord as she crossed the finish line!" They say. "It flew behind her like a victory flag. So she named it Victoria. Isn't that an empowering story?"

No, but good for her.

All joking aside, if your body bounced back perfectly from birth, I'm actually super happy for you. That's cool. You should be proud of yourself, and I'm going to need you to wear extra bikinis in honor of those of us who don't want to.

For the rest of us, though…what the hell, amiright? With so many crazy changes occurring within the one body we have, you'd think someone would've warned us with a billboard or something.

I mean… we're always told about the weight gain, and there are little cutesy jokes about how you pee when you sneeze.

"Har dee har, I sneeze and a little dribble of pee comes out and I laugh and the kids laugh and it's not awkward at all. We've even come up with a cute little name for it: We call it "peezing." Isn't that cute?"

NO. No it isn't cute. Because you don't just leak when you sneeze. Sometimes, you just leak because you waited too long to go the bathroom. Sometimes, this happens when you're hanging out with friends or standing in line at the store. And, I do not care who you are, the moment it happens there will be a split second where your eyes will widen and you'll freeze just a little. If anyone catches that split second, they will ask you what is wrong, and then you'll have to lie. Unless it's another mom. Then she'll just be like, "You peed, didn't you?"

But we're not warned about so much more. General aches and pains and other shit are left up to us to discover like some sort of sick Easter egg hunt. For example, I wasn't told that my stomach muscles could literally stretch until they were unable to fully rejoin. That's called *Diastasis Recti*, and it's a fun one. The sad part of it is, at least in my experience, there are very few doctors who are well-versed in this. It's like the Voldemort of women's issues. It won't be named or mentioned in conversation ever. You'll just wake up one day to realize that your stomach makes a literal triangle when you sit up, and you'll think "that's not a thing I could do before." You'll then find out that the only way to really fix it is by surgery, and even then, nothing is ever really back to where it was. You become a teddy bear someone ripped all of the stuffing out of, then shoved back in all willy-nilly.

In fact, this reminds me of another thing no one warned me about: Namely, that everyone seems to have an opinion on what you should expect from your postpartum body.

After your body becomes yours once more, you'd think you'd finally be in charge of it again without having to worry about other people's comments. You'd think you'd get to decide how you feel about it or what you want to do with it, but you only get to listen to more voices, and more opinions that you didn't ask for. Either you'll be told that you should be totally in love with all of the changes your body has undergone, or you should be covering up all of your mirrors and running endless miles to get in shape. You can't feel okay about some things and want to change others. You can't want to get plastic surgery on a couple things and still be proud that you're a parent. I mean…you can, just not without someone, somewhere telling you that motherhood is a gift and you're an ungrateful boil on the ass of society.

If you're not a mom yet and you're reading this, know that you'll also get to hear all kinds of cutesy little platitudes that are meant to make you love your body but actually just make you annoyed with the biological inaccuracies. The worst of these is "you're a tiger who's earned her stripes" when talking about stretch marks.

"But...but tigers don't earn stripes. They're born with them." I said once.

"Oh, Arianna, it's just a saying." My friend said this with the same tone I reserve for when my son is whining at me.

"I get that, but it doesn't make sense. You can be a badass tigress, I'm down for that, but tigers automatically have stripes. It's not an unlocked achievement."

"Do you have to argue everything? Let people enjoy things."

"I'm not saying you can't look at stretch marks as a badge of courage, I just don't get why you have to use a biological feature that – hey, come back here! Where are you going?"

My friends are tolerant saints. I stand by what I said though.

Anyway.

It's kind of frustrating that we shame each other, as if we're not shamed enough. We're all dealing with the pressure of having to fit other people's opinions as well as our own, so you'd think that we'd have a bit more empathy. But n-o-o-o-o-o, we also have to start shaming one another for not wanting the same things out of our bodies. Some of us want to work out, some of us don't. Some of us (read: me) fucking love bread and want to eat bread and think we should be allowed to be happy because the little baby pouch ain't going anywhere anyway. It pretty much always depends. This isn't just a body image thing. We have a really bad habit of wanting our way to be the only way, especially in parenting. I'll get more into this later, but for now, sticking with the body stuff, "if I can do it, you have no excuse" isn't the best way to keep us from making comparisons.

So we don't allow one another to have our own views on our post baby bodies. You'll either be told that you could be better, or you'll be told that you shouldn't expect better. You're not really allowed to like some things about your body and not others. It's all well-meant, but in a world where we're already told what to do about literally everything, it's just one more thing we have to worry about being judged for.

So in case you need to hear it: Becoming a mother doesn't mean that you suddenly must love, or want to fix, all facets of your body. Despite what seems to be popular opinion, not exactly being thrilled that your boobs are different sizes isn't a form of ungratefulness. You can still be elated to have children, and you can still be proud of your station as a mother, without being 100% in love with all of the physical changes it brings. That's probably my least favorite assumption of all the ones we're hit with. And there are many.

Your relationship with your postpartum body is yours, as long as you're not hurting yourself or anyone else. Highlight that sentence, because you won't hear it much.

You're welcome.

Parenthood can't be fair.

It was always important to me that I have a "50/50 partnership" when I got married. I wanted my husband and myself to split the duties perfectly down the middle. I'd wash the dishes, he'd dry. I'd sweep the floors, he'd mop. I'd change a dirty diaper, he'd slam dunk it into the nearest trashcan. We'd be the perfect, even partners. This was my dream.

It was a stupid dream.

It took me exactly three late-night breastfeedings to realize that, after kids, there is no such thing as a 50/50 partnership. That hope goes the way of the Dodo and there isn't shit you can do about it.

I remember that, when this dawned on me, I was sitting up with my son, slowly removing bits of his clothing to keep him from falling asleep while he was eating (I just want to stress that he was a newborn at the time – otherwise this sentence is really fucking weird). I was angry. I was tired and pissed at my husband, because as I breastfed by the light of my phone's flashlight, he snored on in REM-fueled bliss. I remember glaring down at his stupid face and wanting to throw the stupid baby at his head and tell him to do the stupid feeding so that I could, for once, get some rest.

And then reason cautiously poked its head in and asked me how, exactly, my husband was supposed to help. The baby wasn't taking a bottle yet, and my husband's nipples were purely decorative. I suppose he could have sat up to keep me company, but that would only feed my spite, and it would leave us without anyone fit to run the house the following day. I was on my own because I was the only one who could do that one thing. There was no 50/50 to be had. I was only able to find solace in my son delatching mid-stream and spraying milk all over my sleeping spouse, to which my husband responded by sputtering and waking just enough to mumble "I dreamed it was raining" before rolling over and falling back to sleep.

Another kid and multiple years later, it's still not any closer to that perfect midpoint. This is never really talked about as openly as it should be. You get to hear that either 1) You should be thrilled to be doing whatever you're doing, because you chose to have kids, or 2) that a 50/50 partnership is the key to marital and motherhood bliss. Those seem to be the only two outlooks out there, and I feel like it might maybe perhaps sorta be leading us into this place of dissatisfaction.

The truth is, we can't have a 50/50 partnership, because someone is always going to be more tired, busier, and/or sicker than the other. Chances are, at least one of you will inevitably have eight hours of your day sucked up by a job, so it'll fall on the other partner to handle the non-job stuff, be it dinner or bedtime stories or discipline. If one of you travels, you'll be in charge of everything for multiple days at a time, and it won't end when your partner returns. Even if both of you work outside the home, one of you will have a greater commitment to the parenting gig, which gives you no sick days, minimal vacation days, and no mental health days. One of you will have a schedule that is switched around more often, and that is more dependent on the schedules of everyone else. One of you will be the one most often expected to sacrifice time or energy when time or energy needs to be sacrificed. It will be no one's fault, but it'll feel like it should be somebody's.

If you're not careful, you'll start feeling resentful. You'll start feeling like it's time for comparison. Then, inevitably, you'll wind up having the "Who Does More for the Household" argument.

I'm going to digress to warn you to never ever, no matter how angry you get, have this argument. If you haven't already, good. Don't. Strike the very thought from your brain. Nobody wins, everyone comes out feeling unappreciated and invalidated, and grudges are inevitably held. No good ever comes from this argument; I can promise you this because I unfortunately know from experience.

I don't bring this up to bring you down; rather, I'm about to tell you how I deal with this every day, because I totally get that it's hard as hell to put up with. I'm not perfect at it, but I've gone from wanting to run away forever to only wanting to run away for a couple days, so I think that what we're doing is working. Here's how you deal with the lack of 50/50:

1.   Accept it

Half of you probably just yelled "Arianna, you dick!" and I'm actually okay with that.

Part of what held me back was my inability to give up on the idea of parenthood being fair and equal. If I had to stay up with a sick kid one night, I felt that it was only fair that it be my husband's turn the next night. If I had to run bath time on Monday, it should be his turn on Wednesday. This is a noble thought, but I learned quickly that it wasn't always going to work like that. If he had work the next day, it made more sense for me to sit up with the sick kid an extra night. If he's out of town for business for the next week, I can't just refuse to bathe my kids until he returns. Well, I could, but I hear that's frowned upon and my kids always seem to want to crawl on me when they smell like ass, so I won't.

One of the most helpful things I've ever been told was that we need to keep in mind that it isn't that we *can't* do some things; it's that we *don't want to*. We don't want to be the only one in charge for days or weeks on end. We don't want to have to carry more than what an equal share would be. None of this is anything we're hoping for in the slightest, but it's something we can do, and that's the important part. It often feels like total bullshit that we have to, I know, but a lot of parenthood feels that way.

Point being, for some of this, it's just the way life is. You're not going to be able to force fairness into parenthood, because most of us in most of the world's countries don't have the option. Once you realize that you're going to have to sacrifice your health and your sleep and your sanity sometimes, it will change your mindset. It won't make you happy by any means, and it won't make the situation any more fun, but it'll keep you from feeling resentful, because you'll realize that this shit just is, and it's no one's fault. Just as with anything, the moment you adjust your mindset, things get a little easier. Then you can move on to step two:

2. Make it fair where you can.

In my writings for NYAM, I've made no secret of the fact that I hated staying at home with my kids initially, and that it had absolutely nothing to do with my kids. It had way more to do with the fact that I was stuck in the house all the time with a maybe once-a-month chance to go out and do something for myself. My children were my life, and that never works out well for me. Things only looked brighter when I told my husband outright that some things would need to change. I was going to need time to myself sometimes, my mental health was going to have to become more of a priority for us both, and I was going to need a break of some sort when he got back from business trips.

To be fair, my husband was never averse to any of this. He's a really nice guy — like so nice that I sort of wonder why he's even married to me sometimes — So his response to my conditions was "ok." And he's done a pretty great job of maintaining that.

So I'm not saying it'll be as easy for everyone else, but it totally might be; you especially won't know if you've never tried. Make it a priority for you to find places where you can lighten your load, even in small ways. Even if it's just splitting dish duty, or asking someone else to read the bedtime story while you space out for a second.

If you're not in a partnership, this goes for you, too: you shouldn't be hitting mental walls and having breakdowns constantly. Access the help you can from teachers, friends, and the community. Make things easier wherever you can.

You may very well feel guilty over it, but fuck that noise. You're fine. The next time that you're covered in someone else's bodily fluids and realizing you haven't slept well in the past three days, you'll realize how much you needed that break. There's nothing wrong with asking for help.

And last, but certainly not least:

3.   Don't let anyone else define what "fair" is to you.

You know what people love to have opinions about? Shit that isn't their business. Especially if said shit is your marriage and your parenting.

When you're trying to figure out a balance that works for you and your family, there will be opinions. These opinions will range from "you're putting your kid in daycare when you stay home? How does it feel to be a literal manifestation of Attila the Hun?" to "He should literally be licking your feet and bleaching your asshole. You birthed his child. He owes you."

Fact is, these people all have opinions because the situation isn't theirs to control, so they're totally free from consequence. It's like people who shout plays at their favorite sports teams on TV: They're able to see what "should" be done because a line of 500-pound murder machines isn't running toward them at top speed.

You're the one on the field, and so you're the only person who can decide what's right for you and your family. You. So unless you're really in need of advice, I wouldn't even bother asking for it. Work it out with those who matter, and let everyone else sort their own shit out.

Anyway, I hope that helps, if you're anything like me. If you're not, I just wasted your time. S-o-o-o...sorry. Moving on, here's another thing no one warned me about before I became a parent:

Oh the Hormones!

As my husband once said whilst wrongfully predicting that I was, in fact, not pregnant with my son: "The female reproductive system is a puzzle box. It does kooky things." He was not wrong, though I'm not sure I agree with how his statement makes the uterus sound like a circus.

Before I had kids, I didn't cry at movies. Ever. *Titanic*? Fell asleep on it. *E.T.*? Got bored with it. *Armageddon*? I was too obsessed with Aerosmith's theme song to really get worked up. The only movie that had ever really gotten tears out of me was *The Green Mile*, and even then it was a couple runaway tears that I was able to wipe away before the lights came back on.

Since having kids, I have cried at about five different movies in rapid succession, a Holiday Inn commercial, an episode of *Law & Order: SVU*, the sun shining after two weeks of rain, violins, otters holding hands, and cheese past its expiration date. I am only kidding about some of these, and the horrible thing about hormones is, you have no idea of knowing which ones.

You don't hear much about the hormones and the intensity of their swings, both after you give birth and beyond. Like, we really don't hear as much about Postpartum Depression and Postpartum Anxiety as we should, but at least there's some mention nowadays. Why don't they ever mention the other stuff though? What about the fact that we can sometimes be depressed all day and then completely fine the next for absolutely no reason, sometimes years later? Where were the sex ed lessons about loving someone to the point of almost bursting one second, and then hating the sound of their breathing the next? For ages, I would know it was nine days before my period because I'd go from loving everything to hating existence. I'd feel like crying all day long, and I'd feel overwhelmed by literally everything I was asked to do.

"Arianna," my husband would say, *"would you mind doing the dishes?"*

"WHY DON'T YOU JUST ASK ME TO DIE?!" I'd respond, before throwing a chair and running hysterically from the room.

This happened every month like clockwork. Then I learned about Pre-Menstrual Dysphoric Disorder, or PMDD. I learned about it from an episode of *SVU* (not the same one that made me cry. That show is a roller coaster of emotion for me), not from a doctor or from anyone who is an expert who should've told me about it. Then I found out afterwards just how many women actually dealt with it.

For some reason, a number of women each year find out about birth-related problems – especially hormonal ones – that they never hear about anywhere else. I would tell you a specific number, but it's not particularly easy to find. That's how little research has truly been done on this. The best I could find was a *New York Post* article suggesting that the number of women affected by a hormonal imbalance is nearly 1,000 per 2,000 women aged 30 to 60[1]. An alarming percentage of that thousand doesn't even know how a hormonal imbalance can affect them. Clearly, these things aren't talked about enough. I don't mean that they don't hear about it talked about just in public, or in casual conversation. I mean it's never talked about ever. Not in sex ed, not as they get older, not in birthing classes…NEV-AR. So they don't know about these things until they're fed up enough to insist on being checked by a doctor, which really, really shouldn't be the case. Then, you're not even guaranteed to get a doctor who'll listen to you, because we already know from a number of studies that women are often dismissed when complaining about medical concerns.

Look, I come from a medical family. My father is a doctor. I'm not a fan of believing Google over your family physician. That being said, if you're feeling like you're all over the place or that your body is doing kooky shit—even a few years after having children—you're not even close to alone on this, and you should absolutely look into it when and if you can. One thing I've learned since stretching my body like a balloon twice: You know enough about yourself to at least be able to tell when something's wrong. And if you have to insist that someone look into it, even on a cursory level, insist it. Especially since, postpartum, we're primed and ready for thyroid issues, mental health difficulties, and random aches and pains, amongst other things. Even if there's nothing wrong and we're just doomed to cry at fucking Hallmark movies forever, the least we can do for ourselves is get that shit checked out when we can. Your doctor isn't judging you; your health is their job, and it's important. *You* are important. I will be telling you that many more times throughout this book.

---

[1] M. Haaland. Nearly Half of Women have Been Affected by Hormonal Imbalance. *The New York Post*. 22 Feb. 2019.

Thanks for coming to my TEDtalk.

You will lie to your children like a cheap-ass rug.

It would've been magical if someone could've told me when I was pregnant that all of my notions about being honest with my children would go out the goddamned window the first time I sensed that a lie would get me where I was going faster.

It's hard not to fall into. I mean…you have a goal, and kids — even the brightest kids — are gullible. It takes way more time to have to explain that they need to go to sleep because their brains need to develop and because you need silence so that you can eat a candy bar in the dark without judgement, than it does to say "go to sleep or it'll stay Monday forever." We tend to sense that we have a chance to sway a tender, young brain away from doing shit we don't want, so we lie.

And if you have never, ever, ever lied to your kid ever, that's cool. I mean it. I'm glad. You're probably also an amazing speaker, because you have to explain things a lot. That, or your child is a newborn. In which case, you don't get to say anything until your kid is asking to go out for ice cream and you're stuck between "I don't want to get you any ice cream" and "the ice cream store is closed today."

I'm usually all for honesty, but your kids might not understand why their dead dog isn't really going to a farm upstate. Or they may, but only after you have to answer those hefty questions I mentioned earlier, like "what is death?" and "Do dogs have souls?"

So whatever. What they don't know won't hurt 'em. Or it might. They might be ready to fistfight you one day when they realize the toy store was never really sealed by a magical force field. You've got time until that happens, though – plenty of time to think up an even better lie.

Actually, now that I think about it this is one of the more fun parts of parenthood. Moving on to the next thing:

Nothing you do will ever be good enough. Ever.

I'm not talking about the nasty little voices in our head right now. That comes later.

No, right now I'm talking about everyone looking in from the outside. Those people. They will never be 100% happy with everything you do. You will die first.

Sure, this is a well-known platitude for just about anyone in life, but I feel like parenting has this problem to a special degree. I especially know this, because I was one of those people who thought that people with kids were just being all high-and-mighty when they would tell me that I couldn't understand because I didn't have kids. I thought they were twatwaffles. And maybe they were. But they were right. Also, now that I'm on the other side, I am definitely one of those twatwaffles.

You'll catch shit for any choice you make. Have one kid? Fine, but they're going to grow up selfish. Have five kids? Fine, but that's super irresponsible because you can't possibly watch them all. Punish them for misbehavior? You're not letting kids be kids. Let them off easy? Good job just letting your children walk all over you, ya pansy. And however you choose to handle the work/childcare situation? You can't win that one either.

This one especially pisses me off. I've been a stay-at-home mom, a working mother, and now I'm stay-at-home parenting and working from home. None of this seems to be enough to stop the barrage of idiotic observations from people. It's honestly like diarrhea of the mouth for them.

If you stay at home, you'll get to hear at least once that you don't work. Not that you don't have a job, which is true, but that you don't work. You'll get to hear about how much everyone would love to "get to stay home all day and play with kids." They will make comments about how they'd totally do what you were doing if they could "just get someone else to pay the bills." And they'll always say this with the air of someone who's sharing an in-joke of some sort. Like you're supposed to laugh or throw your hands up in the air all, "you got me! My life is just fun, fun, fun. Sorry, sucker."

If you work outside the home and your child is receiving childcare, people assume that you miss your kid all day long, and that you regret putting them in childcare in the first place. And don't you ever, ever mention that you like working outside of the home, because they'll look at you like you murdered a puppy in front of them, and then they'll ask you if you're sure. As if you might have just had some sort of stroke and forgotten where you stand on your own opinion of things.

My working from home with children seems to be working out well for most people, except I get comments fairly often about "leaving my kids alone." To be fair, there is a lot more independent play time when I have shit to do, because…I mean…I have shit to do. Sometimes there are TV days. This isn't the case every day, but it is a thing. In my defense, working from home with your kids in the house is damn near fucking impossible because my kids don't know how to do anything except try to unplug my stuff and hide my important paperwork. One time, my son even saw fit to hide my glasses in our couch, which doesn't exactly bode well for getting any work done. As you'd imagine, this isn't a productive way to live, so I make them go away for a bit sometimes. This is also not acceptable to some, as I should apparently be playing with them and taking them on Mary Poppins adventures all day. The worst part is, sometimes – more times than should be acceptable – this shit comes from the mouths of other parents.

Side note: Who are all these people whose parents baked them cookies and wiped their asses and stared into their eyes from sunup to sundown? Where are they, and how much are they paying their lobbyists? Most people I know had parents much like mine, who gave me a sibling just so I could annoy someone else for a few hours. So where is the assumption coming from that it's only good parenting if you're dedicating every moment to child-rearing?

Anyway.

You will want to argue with these people. You will want to defend and you'll want to prove and you'll want to argue. Don't. You're wasting your time, because no one is trying to actually learn why you're doing the things you do. No one is trying to understand. Their opinions aren't for you, so much as they're to bolster their own surety in themselves and their own choices. You're merely their emotional punching bag, so just unhook yourself and let them swing at empty air.

No matter which way you go with life, you won't win. So I'm telling you what I wish someone had just told me from the beginning: Do whatever the hell works for you, or for your family, because that's the only time you have a hope of reaching 100% approval.

Last but not least, I'm going to tell you this:

You can read all the books you want and ask all the questions you please, but you will N-E-V-ER truly know what you're in for.

By all means, stalk all the mom blogs and vlogs you want. Ask whoever catches your attention. Read as many books by sarcastic, acid-tongued asshole moms as you want. Your child will sense when you are getting close to understanding their quirks, and then they will change it the fuck up. You will never really know how to handle anything, and they can sense that like sharks sense blood in the water. No matter how much you read, nothing will ready you for the amount of worrying and calculating and juggling you'll do. The weird thoughts that run through your head -- wondering whether or not your child is as smart as other kids or as fast or a strong – will come, no matter how "ready" you think you are for them.

Which is why I sincerely want to tell every person who spews the "you can't complain because you chose to have kids" diatribe to go to hell. I also want you to ignore that lie. Ignore it like it's your kid telling you some long, rambling story while you're trying to zone out and finish your snack. Just as with any major lifestyle change – be it moving to another city, making a major financial decision, or entering into a serious relationship – you took a chance. You went in what felt like the right direction for you, and while you can study up on possible scenarios all you want, life is just too faceted of a thing for you to know all of what might come your way. You might hate the new city you move to. The person you're dating probably pees in the shower. Shitty surprises are going to be everywhere, and the choice being yours doesn't erase the fact that you'll have some adapting and some venting to do. It doesn't mean that you aren't appreciative, or that you don't deserve to be a parent – it only means that you're getting the full experience, the good and the bad. And with kids, the bad can literally be anything. You can never, ever, be ready for everything a choice will throw at you – raising kids least of all.

You won't be ready for how much you'll love them, or how much you'll hate them. You won't be ready for how much kids fucking cost, both in money and in time. You won't even be ready for how slowly they do everything, especially when you have places to be. You will never be on time again and nothing can make that clearer than being in the foxhole yourself. You will never feel fully adjusted to parenting struggles, not even when you've been doing it for decades — trust me, I've asked.

I say this because I don't want you reading this or any other book and then expecting your children to suddenly make sense to you. Instead, I'd rather that you approach every situation like a puzzle that needs solving. Assume that each puzzle has different pieces. Maybe it's even missing pieces. And the picture on the box isn't even for the puzzle that you're working on. Figure it out according to that moment. If you don't do that, the moment that your usual solution doesn't work, you're going to beat yourself up. Then you're going to allow other people to beat you up. And the truth is, as I'm sure you've gathered, other people barely have themselves figured out most days; they're sure as hell not going to know a thing about you.

That is all.

4

On Sex and Sexuality

Before I begin, I want to say two things. Firstly, my mother is probably reading this book. She's always had a rather open, healthy attitude towards sex, and she was always very honest with me and my brother about sexual health. That being said, I'm sure she probably got all squinchy-faced at the idea of having to read a chapter about my feelings on sex. So…I dunno…sorry, Ma.

Secondly, while I consider myself to be a rather open person regarding sex and the like, please know that I'm not saying that we should suddenly start asking our mothers and grandmothers about their sex lives, because that's just weird and gross. Naturally, we don't want to know about those kinds of things because we're not meant to be titillated by the idea of our family members feverishly humping away at each other. That's not judgment; it's evolution. So don't feel guilty if you still would like to pretend you were born by Immaculate Conception, because no one wants to have to think about their family doing the Horizontal Mambo surrounded by candles and listening to Marvin Gaye. No one should have to. Except my mother, apparently. Don't feel sorry for her, though – when you think about it this is kind of her fault.

Alright. Now that we've gotten that over with, let's dive in.

If you're hoping for a well thought-out, scientific approach to sex/sexuality/sexiness in motherhood, I'm going to assume you just opened the book to this page. How unlucky for you. I'm not really going to quote very many statistics in this chapter, because I don't think lack of research is the problem. Rather, I think we can look at all the studies and numbers and percentages we want, but at some point, we have to just acknowledge what we see: Everyone thinks that our naughty bits shrivel up the moment we have children – even us, to a degree -- and it's harshing our buzz.

So, don't get me wrong: I'm not about to tell you that this is all about your mindset, and that if you just want sex a little harder, it'll happen more often. I'm not going to pretend that there aren't things out there that we wouldn't be caught dead in nowadays, because I, too, have noticed that crop tops quit being my friend after college. What I am going to tell you is, it's not gross or weird or inappropriate to like sex after you've had a kid. It's not weird to need a break from it after you've had a kid. And you damn sure don't quit being sexy just because you've given birth. And, while I get that it's sometimes very hard not to feel like things have changed for the worst in this department, I think we owe it to ourselves to accept that sex is still a part of most of our lives. After all, your kid didn't get here by magic – someone had to bump uglies to get them here.

But I'm getting ahead of myself. Let's take these one at a time, shall we? We shall.

You're still sexy. That's not weird.

I find it unfair that parents aren't allowed to be comfortable in their own sensuality. Like, we're supposed to be hot enough to get people to want to make babies with us, and then once that baby exists, we're expected to just shut that shit off. No matter how much we oozed sex beforehand – I didn't, but I'm sure some of you out there did – we're no longer supposed to celebrate that once kids enter the picture. It's idiotic, but it's so ingrained that we don't even think twice about it.

My favorite example actually involves a celebrity, Jenna Dewan. If you just said "who?" It's fine. I only know who she is because she was married to Channing Tatum, who may or may not be a marble statue come to life, and I was low-key jealous of her. You don't have to know who she is. That part doesn't matter.

What does matter is that Jenna one day posted a photo of herself on the internet. This woman is a dancer and a model, and she has money and she has time. All of these things together resulted in what I believe the kids are calling "a bangin' body," despite having just ejected a daughter from it. She looked fantastic, and she wanted to show it off one day with lingerie that hugged her in places I forgot even existed on us. And you know what? The photo was fucking stunning. She was on a balcony and the sun was shining on her, and she looked great. I remember looking at that photo and actually feeling secondhand pride, because girlfriend looked like she felt alive and human and beautiful, and dammit, that's how we all should feel.

Then I read the comments and remembered why social media is both a blessing and a curse.

Assuming this isn't being read in a post-apocalyptic future wherein the robots finally got sick of our shit and revolted, you know how the internet can be a double-edged sword. Everyone gets to have a voice, but also, *everyone* gets to have a voice. Even people who probably should've had their tongues removed by nature generations ago. And, in poor Jenna's situation, the law of numbers dictated that she wound up with a more-than-healthy dose of opinions from those people. The same stupid sentiment was repeated over and over again, just with different words: "why is she posing like this? Isn't she a mom? She should be ashamed of herself."

This went on for pages with very little originality thrown in. To be fair, there were people trying to stand up for her, asking people what the hell their problem was and telling them to shut up, but this shouldn't have been a conversation in the first place. And yet…there it was. It was bizarre, because we all know damn well that if Jenna hadn't had any children when she posted that photo, the majority of people would have probably just talked about how fantastic she looked. The moment we threw kids into the mix, though, a woman owning her own sexuality was a problem.

The more I thought about it, though, the more I realized that we don't exactly help our cases. Mothers, I mean. In fact, some of the people ripping on poor Jenna were sure to mention that they were mothers themselves.

"I have three children," they'd say, "and I'd never let little Jacsun, Pacsun, and Smacksun see me dressed like this. She should have some dignity."

Dignity. What a word. It was thrown around a lot in those comments, and I personally don't feel that we, people who have had people gathered around our goddamned vaginas at least once in our lives, should be lecturing anyone on dignity. The moment kids came into our lives, that word was forever redefined. Notice I never said it was gone, just changed. So we need to stop expecting the old definition to apply to us.

We do this all the time: We suddenly scoff at the idea of wearing lingerie or being attractive to anyone ever. We scowl at women – especially other mothers – who don't seem to have this problem and dress in ways that draw eyes, as if motherhood suddenly means we're all supposed to fade into the background and become a part of the decor. We watch women partying or dancing suggestively and snort at them.

"She needs to grow up. She's a mother now."

To which the only good reply is: Yeah? So? She feels great, you control where your eyes go, and unless you're paying her you don't get to enforce a goddamned dress code.

There's a lot going on here, and it all comes down to a cycle we've got to break. We get all weird because we're too busy basing our perceptions on our impressions of our own mothers. Our own mothers were asexual creatures who merely existed to get us cereal and wipe our asses, so that's what we should be. Even if this doesn't make us feel too great once we're in the Mommy Seat, even if it doesn't sync with our perceptions of ourselves, we assume the identity because then we'll be just like one of the most important people in our lives – or so we believe. Then we get pissed or feel funny when other moms don't do this, because it challenges shit we swore we knew.

So I'm going to tell you two things that are horribly important here:

1: Your mom was still totally having sex and/or masturbating when you were a kid, and

2: She didn't stop being a woman just because you entered her life. She changed, sure, but she remained a woman with needs and a self-image.

I'm going to assume that you went to go scrub your eyes with steel wool after the first point, so I won't elaborate on that any further.

The second point is really the most important one, because it affects every mother out there, including you. It's simple, really: we need to start challenging the belief that we stopped being human the moment we had children.

We can't be the only ones blamed for this. It's not like we don't also have advertisements and TV shows and just about every other fucking thing telling us that motherhood means we're virginal, sexless beings who only exist to kiss scraped knees and whip up weird casseroles. It's there in the terms they use to describe the things we use and/or wear day to day, like "mom jeans," "mom haircut," and "mom mobile": All meant to compare us to things that are boxy, uncool, unflattering, and nonthreatening. We're told that we're supposed to be "modest" now (whatever the hell that means) for our children's sakes, so that they can follow our shining examples. We belong to our children, and therefore all of our needs, urges, and great hair days now come second or third to everything else.

Fuck that. Bold it, put it in caps, underline it, and italicize it. Oh wait, I can do that myself:

FUCK. THAT.

You know what motherhood is? It's a role, a new job title to put on your life's resume. It's a new part of who you are and a new part of your personality, but it does not replace who you were once before. You're allowed to celebrate your body however you see fit, because that's a right all women – all human beings—have, and you're still a human being, just with at least one other, younger human being around who gets up in your face a lot. Despite any physical or physiological changes to them, you still have the same arms, legs, head, and heart that you had before and during your pregnancy. So don't let anyone make you feel like you're not a damned person anymore.

I guess what I'm saying is, if you've got it, flaunt it if you want. If you have the urge, feed it. Don't be afraid to talk about it with friends, and if that's not your style, don't get shitty with someone else who's comfortable with it. There's no shame in maintaining your own level of modesty, as long as you let others do the same. And don't use motherhood as a tool to try to suppress and shame yourself or others just because there are broken people out there who believe you should. Instead, reframe what motherhood is in your head, and understand that your wants and needs as a woman don't suddenly disappear in a puff of smoke, and that's okay. In fact, that's normal. Anyone who tries to make you feel bad for wanting sex, talking about sex, having a giant collection of scary-looking and horribly powerful vibrators, whatever…they're the ones who have it all wrong, not you.

Your body may be different from how you remember, but I promise you that if you gave yourself the chance, you'd find so much about it that's still beautiful. And that beautiful body still deserves the most enthusiastic of lovin', no matter how many kids you've got.

That being said, I'm about to give you whiplash, because:

You may not want sex as much anymore. This is common.

Since having children, I'm tired all of the time. I'm sure you can relate.

I have a theory that children are tiny vampires who feed on energy instead of blood. When you first wake up in the morning, those "hugs" they give you are actually them sucking up energy you've stockpiled so that they can jump off your furniture and ask you for snacks every 30 seconds. It's the only way that I can explain how children get up before we do, but are still zooming around the room right before bedtime while we're lying on the floor like rugs, wondering why our own bedtime is still four hours away.

You know what's not fun when you're tired? Sex. I mean, if that's your kink or whatever, I'm not shaming you. You do you. But I like to actually be involved in the process, and it's not at all fun for either me or my husband when just the thought of thrusting makes me want to sleep for the rest of my life. I still remember my husband trying to initiate once after a day of running after children and trying to stay awake.

"Fine." I said. "Is it okay if we do it in a position where I don't have to move too much?"

Suffice it to say that sex didn't happen that night. Turns out requesting that I get to lie there like a limp fish kills the mood. I got sleep though, so score for me.

Parenting brings in new issues that can mess with any frisky feelings you might have. Postpartum, you generally tend to feel extremely tired, on top of dealing with organs moving back into place, hormones making you crazy, just about every damn thing making you farty, and your mirror reminding you every day that you've got some changes to get used to. When they're a little older, you're struggling with having the energy to keep up with your kids, to satisfy every single responsibility you have, and to find time to take care of yourself. As time goes on, you can add worrying about your kids' wellbeing, worrying about money, not taking enough vacations, and watching yourself age five years every time your family does something stupid.

It's a lot. With that much going on, sex is often the last thing on your mind, and that's completely understandable. I don't think I need to tell you that a majority of people see a sharp decline in sexual interest after having kids. I know I said I wasn't going to bring numbers into it, but I lied. A study done in 1986 found that as high as 60% of couples were having less sex after a year of parenthood[2] , so I mean…it hasn't exactly been a mystery. My problem with it, though, is that I feel like we're still made to feel bad if we're not foraging the energy from God-knows-where to be physically available for our partners, no matter what we're dealing with at the time.

Frankly, I'm rather sick of how many things I see out there blaming us for not wanting to be touched. We're told that we need to change our mindsets; that we need to fix ourselves; that we need to remember why we liked doing it in the first place, etc. as if we're the only ones responsible in the first place for getting to a place where we've forgotten. And maybe we didn't forget; maybe we think about how much fun it was all the time. But the thing is, our responsibilities have changed, and now "fun" sounds like a lot of work. For some reason, we aren't allowed to acknowledge that.

So how about we acknowledge it now? How about we admit that we're busy, that a lot of shit falls on our shoulders to get done, and that it's understandable that, sometimes, we might be stretched too thinly to feel sexual? How about we admit that, if we want that to change, it's not just our fault? Instead of picking up books geared just at us -- telling

---

[2] Fischman, S., Rankin, E., Soeken, K., Lenz, E. Changes in Sexual Relation-ships in Postpartum Couples. *Principles and Practice,* Jan/Feb 1986, pp.58-63.

us how to feel sexy again or how to reclaim our womanhood so we can give our partners mind-blowing orgasms as if we're just little broken sex machines, -- we finally allow ourselves to believe that it's OK to be tired? Then we can accept the truth adjacent to that: there's more tied to your libido than just a simple "mindset adjustment," and it's cool to make adjustments to other things in order to get closer to where you'd like to be.

That could mean talking to your partner about the things you need to feel more sexually comfortable. It could mean pulling in a third party to help you better understand where your relationship could use a little balance (like a therapist or a counselor is what I mean…though if you want to do the other thing you'll get no judgement from me). Besides cheating or …I dunno…murder…your methods should be whatever works. As long as you get to a point where sex is a thing you have the energy for and not just another item on your to-do list, you're golden.

And yes, if you've been following, I've done podcast episodes with amazing women and coaches who suggests things like planning sex, flirting, and making an effort to have great sex. I still maintain that for you to even get to the point where you want to do those things, you have to have the energy. And in order for you to have that, you'll need to free up that energy in the first place. Ultimately, sex and sexual desire is a concerted effort between both parties. It can involve reconnecting with yourself both emotionally and physically, but it can also involve your partner doing more than just asking you if you have five minutes to touch their genitals. There are many things that can play into a sudden disinterest in sex; we just need to be told way more often that we aren't the only variable.

And after all that, even if you're still too tired sometimes, that's still ok.

Until the kids grow up and move out, that's kind of how it's going to be.

On the flip side of this…

You may still actually like sex. That's awesome.

Personally, I very much enjoy sex. I always have. I think that's the whole point. There are actually many moms out there who still enjoy it and make time for it. And not the afternoon quickies you fit in between the kids' naptime and snack. The good kind of sex. Sexy sex. The kind that's sexual.

OK I'll stop. My point still stands though.

Women are shamed for enjoying sex as it is, but if you're a mother who doesn't fear talking about it, or who approaches it with actual excitement? Forget it. What the hell are you doing? You have children. Act like a woman and keep that shit to yourself. Grow up.

I don't get that attitude in the slightest. If you've had biological children without any fertility aids, you had to have sex to have them. If you didn't, I mean…once you get to a certain age, it's kind of assumed that you've seen someone naked in a sexual capacity. Why in the world are we supposed to pretend that it isn't something that we do, much less something that we like?

So I'm not going to get into the long, feminist rant that I could get into about this, because I think we all know that when it comes to society's attitude towards sex-positive women, the deck is pretty well stacked against us. We all already know that we're expected to become Snow White-Betty Crocker-nun amalgams the moment a kid comes out of our butt (that's where kids come from, right? We're also not really supposed to be knowledgeable about our own bodies or reproductive health, so I'm not sure). We know all of this already, so instead, I'm going to focus on something else. Instead, I'm going to say this:

If you're reading this passage and you still really like sex: That is fantastic, good for you.

If you're reading this passage and you don't: As I've mentioned, that is also fine, but you've got to quit acting like the women who do are weird or over-the-top. It ain't exactly helping our cause.

I've actually seen this in person. A group of women I know were all discussing sex one day, and they were going on about positions they didn't like and things they'd never tried. The conversation turned to anal sex. I do not know why, but I have had a weird number of talks amongst girlfriends about anal sex. It is not the way the conversation starts, but for some reason, we always seem to get there.

During this conversation amongst friends, it became pretty clear that most of the women in our group didn't have particularly positive views on sex. It was tiring when they were already tired, it was hard to focus when they already had 9,000 things to do…just about everything in the section before this one seemed to be a pain point. Well, that and the fact that every one of us seemed less than enchanted with butt stuff. Then one of the women, who'd been pretty silent up until that moment, chimed in:

"Actually, I really enjoy anal sex."

Silence. Then the group erupted into surprise and confusion. As more was asked, it turned out that this woman actually enjoyed a whole host of things that had been complained about during that conversation; in fact, she clearly, on the whole (heh…h ole) enjoyed sex very much. Then another of us came out and mentioned that she had a pretty crazy libido herself. The words "multiple times in a day" were bandied about, which made me feel tired just thinking about it.

It stuck with me later how incredulous the others became at the suggestion that two other mothers might want to actually have sex or be sexually adventurous with their spouses. They weren't upset or grossed out, to be clear, but they were surprised. This is part of the problem. It's normal for us to complain about sex, to complain about the fact that our partners want sex, and to talk about how we're too tired for sex. It's become completely acceptable to be the clichéd tired mom who would rather sleep than be touched. This has become so commonplace, in fact, that we're convinced that the opposite doesn't exist. After all, who has the time to even think about these kinds of things?

The answer, surprisingly, is more than we think. Peanut, a mom-friend matching app, did a study of 1,000 moms recently and found that over 61 percent of them wished they were having more sex[3]. Well over half of one thousand women aged 22 to 37 were randy and ready to go, but had things (read: all of life) in the way.

"But wait, Arianna," you say, pausing in strengthening your Kegels, "you said just a little ago that 60% of people aren't having sex. How can the same number not be having it, but also be wanting it?"

Well, my friend, it's simple: Most of us still want sex. We're just dealing with a lot of things that get in the way. And as mentioned already, those things won't get fixed until we stop putting the entire burden on ourselves to do so. You know that saying "it takes two to tango?" Well, you also need two to fix the routine when it falls out of step. And you need to be honest enough to bring in an instructor when you've forgotten the sequence. Man, I am good at dance metaphors. I bet you're impressed.

Fantastic wordplay notwithstanding, it's totally fine to love doing the horizontal mambo. The only thing that isn't fine is others making you feel strange for admitting it. You do you, boo. That's the whole damned point.

If you take nothing else from what I've said thus far, I want you to take these three things:

1.   Your attitude towards your body and towards sex are your own. They're not weird or wrong. They are what they are.

2.   It is not just your responsibility to prioritize sex in your relationships. Communication, cooperation, and honesty with yourselves and each other are key. It's a two-person job. And...

3.   You never stopped being sexy or sexual; anyone who's told you otherwise is lying. You can own it if you want to, or you can choose not to. But your role as a mom isn't what makes that decision for you. You

---

[3] Peanut. Inside the Secret Sex Lives of Millennial Moms. Aug 2018. https://www.peanut-app.io/millennialmomsurvey

got here with sex. Your children got here with sex. And, as hard as it is to believe, if you want grandkids, they will have to get here the same way. So we really, really need to quit acting like this stops being a reasonable part of life after it results in children.

Anyone who tells you otherwise can go fuck themselves.

Pun 100% intended.

And one more thing…

Quit trying to make that "old spark" happen. It's not gonna happen.

The whole idea of "regaining the old spark that you once had," or whatever the shit it is, is so damaging, and I'm here to tell you that spark is gone. I'm not saying that you and your partner aren't still into each other. I'm just saying that the dynamic has changed. It should change. You're now at least one kid's Snack Bitch; that sort of changes things.

I get the need to reclaim old feelings; it's intoxicating when you first meet each other, right? You smile, they smile, you trade some adorable anecdotes and giggle at each other's jokes, and then you go home and excitedly finger each other's buttholes until sunrise. Then you realize you're crazy about each other and decide that you could play with each other's buttholes every day for the rest of your lives. You're always making eye contact with one another and sending cutesy messages that say things like "I can't stop thinking about you." That whole thing is addicting past the level of most narcotics, so it's totally understandable that we'd want to chase it for the rest of our relationship's lifespan.

Then you have kids, and you're tired a lot, and sex often happens within a time limit. You can't laugh at each other's jokes or look into each other's eyes for too long, because there always seems to be a person who needs your attention and will break your shit to get it. Messages look more like "Can you bring home bread, milk, and cheese?" And none of this sounds like the shit romance novels are made of, so we often get to this point and feel like we've failed. We tell ourselves that, if we can just get back to the point where we're ripping each other's clothes off and taking one another like animals, we'll have the perfect relationship.

Yeah, no. Stop that. Once you have children that is not a thing anymore. It shouldn't be.

Love, when first invoked, is a chemical reaction that's meant to be unignorable. It's supposed to get us riled up and ready, because if it doesn't, we don't propagate the species. If we don't propagate the species, the apes take over the earth and we lose. These things are important.

After we propagate –about 18 months afterward—those chemicals dissipate and we start to notice that our partner pees in the shower or chews with their mouth open. We also start realizing that sometimes, we'd rather sleep than hump. We've been told so often by TV and books and experts alike that we're not supposed to feel that, so we assume something's wrong. For some, it might be. For the rest of us, though, we just haven't been told that it's OK to pursue something different now. Like, yeah, you're allowed to still have the urges, but that old spark is…well…old. It's evolved. You've got a new one now. Parent life has seen to that.

"But Arianna," you say, pointing frantically at an old episode of *The Fresh Prince of Bel-Air*, "look at how Uncle Phil chases Aunt Viv upstairs all excitedly to do stuff to her. They're clearly still ready to go, and their kids are grown. And my dad's cousin's maid's cat sitter's brother-in-law and his wife say they still are as in love with each other as the day they met and have sex once a day!"

Uncle Phil and Aunt Viv had something special. Mainly that they were fictional characters, so let's get that part straight first. Next, we should talk about that really weird acquaintanceship you have; like, not everyone's your friend. Have some standards.

Anyway.

To your second point, people can absolutely love each other as much as – or more than—they did from day one and still not do the nasty every day. What you're seeing in those people, though, is not an ability to keep an old flame alive so much as a willingness to embrace and stoke a brand new one as it changes. We haven't been told enough that "new" doesn't necessarily mean "bad." You may not be basking in the roaring fire of your love 'n' shit, but maybe that's because you've got each other to keep warm, so the flames don't need to be as high. It's cool to nurture the new, more natural, less chemically-driven spark rather than trying to go crazy with passion all the time. It's cool to have date nights and decide once in a while that you'd like to just talk and then sleep next to each other, rather than trying to meld into one big, human passion stick. I mention that we're human multiple times – and I'm gonna keep mentioning it – but I'm not going to say we're the exact same human beings, because we're not. You shouldn't be holding anything to a pre-kid standard; not your body, not your mind, and not your relationship.

I mean, also, you'll be in the mood less often because you have kids, and kids exist to fuck your whole shit up. Trying to build a mood? They'll kill it. Making a fancy meal? They'll interrupt it. Giving a sensual, bareback massage? A child will inevitably enter the room, knock the massage oil over onto a candle, and burn your room down. It's not their fault, to be fair; children are just genetically programmed to stop you from having any fun. Have you ever tried to get randy after you've spent all day cleaning their pee and shit from various parts of your floor, your clothing, and from under your fingernails? Immediate boner killer.

Kids also have literally no concept of privacy, making any impromptu sessions you try into a terrifying game of How Long until They Catch Us and We Scar Them for Life. My son walked in on my husband and me recently. It had been a long time since I had touched my husband's wee-wee, and we had an open afternoon. I'd assumed that if my door was locked, my son would be content to watch his tablet and leave us be for a few minutes. I was wrong.

The lock did not work. My son did not leave us alone as I had asked him to. The moment his eyes met mine, the moment I yelled "GET OUT," and the moment he took off running were three of the worst I've ever experienced. I was mortified. My husband got up and just kept testing the lock on the door like it was magically going to show him what went wrong. Then we agreed we'd need to talk to the boy. After we finished up, though, because you only get so much quality time in our situation and I mean…what was done was done.

Upside? The kid remembers that he caught us "wrestling." Downside? He won't quit talking about it, to the point where he felt it necessary to tell his teacher and a neighborhood friend of mine that "Daddy slaps Mommy's booty in bed when they're wrestling." He hasn't let fly with it at a dinner party yet at least, but I'm sure it's coming. That or he's going to get a good look at our Thanksgiving turkey in about a decade, and the stuffing is going to trigger some very complicated memories. I'm not sure and I try not to think about it.

For like four days afterwards, I felt weird even looking my husband in the eye. On top of all the other daily shit that usually gets in the way of feeling amorous or even slightly aroused, I was also struggling with feelings of guilt and shame and being completely without privacy. None of those things make you want to take your pants off; in fact, they make you want to wrap yourself in a parka and stay in a dark room. If you constantly feel like any attempts at sex or intimacy are only going to be interrupted by a baby crying or a sick child or a four-year-old who needs to be taught to knock, you won't ever be in the mood. What's the point?

You're not failing if you admit that kids do make things more complicated. I don't think you should just blame them for everything, but it's very hard to be in a moment that calls for pure attention and emotional connection when a part of you is always on call. If you're finding this to be a problem, not only are you not alone, but it's also completely understandable. I still think it's a road block that you should work around as a team, but it is a road block that legitimately exists. If you're told that it shouldn't be, or that you can "just put them in their rooms and turn the TV on real loud when you've got a second," you have my permission to show them this passage and tell them that Arianna says you're playing Russian Roulette with your naked ass. Do not play Russian Roulette with your naked ass.

In all seriousness, we're constantly wondering whether or not we're doing enough when it comes to all aspects of daily life, and sex is just another thing to throw onto the pile. We shouldn't be worrying about that, because there are extenuating circumstances. These extenuating circumstances walk and talk and go through your drawers and laugh at your attempts at being left alone, so you need to be kind to yourself. It might take a little longer for you, but if you want to get there, you will. I totally think you should look into ways to try.

Just, for the love of all that is holy, make sure you've got a good lock.

5

You're Not Imagining It: It's Hard as Balls to Make Friends as a Parent

Can we just say it already? Making friends as a parent is fucking exhausting.

To be fair, it's tiring even when you don't have kids. Basically, the moment you become responsible for making your own friends, it becomes an exhaustive situation not unlike dating, but without the exhilarative promise of sex afterwards.

Like you remember how you made some friend in high school that was a total waste of time? We all had one. This kid probably had other friends you didn't quite vibe with and liked weird shit for breakfast, like a can of Mountain Dew and dry toast. You remember how you eventually realized that you didn't want to be friends with this person anymore, and that despite the fact that they were the absolute fucking worst, you still felt some pain in your heart from letting them go? And then you remember how you sat down after writing angrily in your poetry journal, tears streaming down your face, and consoled yourself with: *I can't wait until I'm an adult. Making friends will be so much easier when I don't have to deal with high schoolers anymore?*

HAHAHAHAHAHAHAHAHAHAHAHAHAHAHAHAHAHAHAH AHA...

Wait. Wait. Ok I'm good. So...

HAHAHAHAHAHAHAHAHAHAHAHAHAHAHAHAHAHAH
AAAAAAA!

Ah, it feels good to laugh again.

Clearly, as an adult reading this book, you've realized that making friends only gets harder as you get older. No, it isn't just in your head: making friends as an adult – and especially a parent –is harder than we thought it would be by a lot. When you're a kid, you can approach another kid, find out you both like the same cartoons, and then decide to be friends forever. Even in high school, you can fall into a group of friends simply by making the right joke or smuggling the right bottle of booze from your parents' liquor cabinet. Which was wrong of you by the way, because that was probably the liquor your parents drank when they realized they had no friends.

But as an adult, there are so many other things you have to worry about –politics, hygiene, whether or not their house is too far away to drive – without a parent to help you make these decisions. Turns out, getting to know someone beyond a regular "hi" and "bye" takes effort. Who knew?

So that's the bad news.

Here's more bad news: You made it worse by becoming a parent.

Kids muck up the process a bit. How are you supposed to find time for friends when you're expected to be available for on-demand hugs and discipline? And then, of course, there are the last-minute cancellations. We wind up having to cancel plans due to sickness, schedule conflicts, and being too goddamned exhausted to get up once we've sat down, and that also kind of puts a bit of a monkey wrench in things.

Here's kind of good news: At least you're normal.

See, it turns out that according to a few studies out there, one of them via the group Action for Children, about fifty-two percent of parents admitted to feeling lonely[4]. This study was done in 2017, but I think

---

[4] Knapton, S. Parenthood Leaves Half of Mothers and Fathers Feeling Lonely. *The Telegraph*. Nov. 2017.

I'm safe in assuming that this isn't a number that's going anywhere any time soon.

It makes sense that we feel lonely. We didn't have time before we had kids, but now that we're cohabitating with walking Petri dishes who also don't seem to understand that fire is hot and electric outlets are not places to play, we have even less time. We have lessons to drive to, projects to help with, jobs to do, meals to serve, water to drink, workouts to procrastinate on, and massive amounts of Advil to take. Making time for friends is just another to-do that we don't always have energy or patience for. That exhaustion, when added to work or personal projects, makes for a real energy-sucking good time. Isolating ourselves feels a whole hell of a lot better sometimes than making the time to look for, and/or keep up, friendships.

We have to, though. Make time, that is. We hate hearing that so fucking much that I'm certain I've raised some hackles just by saying it. When we hear that we have to make time for something, it feels like someone is insisting that we're not trying hard enough despite the fact that we're trying really hard all day long. Let me be clear: I'm not saying the spirit isn't willing. I'm just saying that I've also noticed that it's popular in many parenting circles to hang out, enjoy each other's company, maybe even get one another's numbers, then go back to their houses and never speak to one another again. Oh, you'll make mention of how you "totally need to hang out sometime," but then you won't do that because you're busy doing other things, and everything else sounds way more important. Eventually, you may even tell yourself that it's the other person's fault for not reaching out first.

"But Adrianna," you say, butchering my name even though for God's sake it's literally right in front of you and there isn't, nor has there ever been, a "d" in it, "time with my family is important, too. And I'm an introvert. And I mean…I already have some friends. I just don't see them often because I'm busy with life."

I'm down with all that you're saying. I get it. Except for the name thing, but whatever. Listen: Much as it probably annoys you to hear it, friendships – the good, life enriching ones – take time and effort before they've even really begun. It's an unfair truth, but there it is.

How much time, you ask? Believe it or not, there have been actual studies done to answer this. The latest of which, at the time of this writing, was done by the University of Kansas. Findings showed that it takes 40 to 60 hours to form a casual friendship; 80 to 100 hours to become friends, and *200 hours* to be considered best, or close, friends[5]. That means you need at least forty hours to feel comfortable asking a friend to borrow a pen you might forget to bring back, and about eight days' worth of time to be certain you want to see each other more than a couple times a year. Hanging out for about two hours at a time means you have to hang out about 100 times on average before you decide you want to be best friends forever. Or, I guess you could be weird and just stay at each other's houses for eight days – only a little bit of judgment there. Point is, if you're not even willing to work for those first five minutes, numbers suggest you're not going to get anywhere.

I wish this study had been around for me a few years ago, because I learned this the hard way.

I lived in Austin, Texas for almost seven years, and I flourished there. I had friends, I had a community, I knew where everything was without a GPS...life was great. Except when it wasn't. My daughter arriving ten days earlier than her due date, and my husband nearly missing her birth, brought to light the fact that it really sucked not having family in the area. We weighed our options for a bit and decided we'd move to the Pacific Northwest, where my husband's family is from. The kids would have cousins, aunts and uncles, and grandparents out that way, and for me there would be no roaches. It was a win-win for everyone.

Except when it wasn't. I've lived my entire happy-ass-life in the South. I like heat. I enjoy walking past friendly strangers and receiving

---

[5] Hall, Jeffrey A. How many hours does it take to make a friend? *Journal of Social and Personal Relationships.* 15 March, 2018. Pp 1278-1296.

a smile and a wave and a comment about my outfit. I like the sun. You know…human things. And the Pacific Northwest doesn't give a damn what I like. It's gray everywhere from November to late June if you're lucky. People are okay with your existence, but they don't particularly revel in it, and roaches are traded for a goddamned yellow jacket season. Because someone in charge of nature looked at the douchebroey-est member of the insect kingdom and thought "there's just not enough of these aggressively sniffing your face for food and trying to sting you in the eye. We need thousands of them for three months straight."

As you've probably already figured, I don't fit in here like I did in the south, and I let it overtake me for a while.

Before we came to settle in Portland, we lived in Seattle for a few months. I mainly wallowed in how busy I was with my kids, with a massive move, and with my brand-spanking-new seasonal depression. I felt lonely and bitter, especially when social media showed me that my old Texas friends were still getting together and talking as if I'd never even left. To me, it looked like they were frolicking through flowers and giggling together while I sat in a tiny basement apartment, getting crawled all over by stir-crazy children. You want to talk lonely? I'd never felt lonelier in my life.

Except at some point, I realized that loneliness is one of the few things in life that can often be worked out of, and I'd need to actually…y'know…try. So I did.

I'm not in any way going to tell you it was easy. It was not. I'm an introverted-ambivert and a bit of an asshole; I do not like to "work the room." I'm more the "hang out by the hors d' oeuvres and hiss when people try to take the crackers I want" type. But I also realized that getting out of the house is crucial to defeating Seasonal Affective Disorder. Having friends would force me to get out of the house. Therefore, I needed friends. So I pasted a smile on my face, tried to appear more open, and I went to work trying to make friends.

A lot of us don't want to be that person who smiles and starts a conversation on the playground, because that person can be rejected. We're right to feel that way, turns out; I felt weird, and I was rejected a lot. Many people either answered me in very short, clipped answers and scurried away, or they just wouldn't respond to my initial smile in their direction in the first place. You know what I realized during all of that, though?

That I was going to die alone and friendless. It felt pretty shitty and I came to no happy epiphanies during that first week. The beginning of the second week, though, was a different story.

I took my kids to a local center to play, and my son ran over to a kid he'd never met in his life to yell "HI! WANT TO PLAY?" like he was rubbing it my face. Of course, the kid agreed. As they ran off into the playroom, flaunting their immediate friendship for all to see, I looked up at the kid's mom and unexpectedly met her gaze. A smile bisected my face, and I felt like a freak. To my shock, though, she smiled back. We said hi, introduced our rude-ass kids to one another, and then the mom walked in with her friends. Something told me in her body language that she was inviting me to stand and talk with them if I wanted to.

I did join them, but I'm not going to say that it was anything you'd aspire to. First, I wandered around the room with my youngest, scoping out the mom and her little group like a shark eyeing a group of fish – or a fish eyeing a group of sharks. Either feels applicable. Then, I slowly made my way closer and closer to the group without saying anything, because in my mind I was handling this like a champ -- a creepy, slow-moving champ. I wanted to give them the chance to either wave me in or stare at me until I slithered away. And then the moment came: The really nice mom, the mom who'd smiled at me, turned her body to open their circle, and asked me a question directly. I became one of their fold.

The rest of the conversation went normally, and I felt excited to be standing in a group of friendly moms who also all seemed pretty down-to-earth and inclusive. I felt lucky. Except I realized later that I wasn't lucky – I had put in the work. As awkward as it may have been, I made the effort to say "hello," and it had finally worked out. That's when I had that epiphany I mentioned earlier: Every friendship begins with a greeting. People like being greeted. They like knowing that you're interested in their friendship. Even if they scurry away or seem uninterested in making friends at the time, the problem isn't with you putting yourself out there; it's with something going on inside them. We're social creatures, and we're programmed to like the flattery of a friendly "hello." As I just demonstrated, it doesn't even have to be a smooth or exciting "hello." Short of randomly putting their fingers in your mouth or something, any greeting or show of friendship will do it. Think of it this way: if someone chooses not to spend their time on you, you've gained the knowledge that they weren't worth it anyway. You only have something to gain from being open and kind – you have nothing to actually lose.

To be clear: I mean open and kind with a smile and wave, not with your wallet or whatever. So no one send me any emails like "I listened to you, Arianna, and now this guy owns the deed to my house and I'm wearing a beer case because he took all my clothes!" I didn't tell you to do that. All I'm saying is friendship starts with a nicety, and you're not hurting yourself by being the first one to extend that. So do that.

If this sounds too easy to be true, it is. After that greeting, after that initial introduction, you have to follow-up. This, more than anything else, has proven to be a struggle for many parents I know. We're excellent at the lead up, but the moment we have to actually make the time to reach out again, we get lazy. The arguments of being "too busy" or "too tired" start rolling off of our tongues again, and the next thing we know we're complaining a month later that we wish we had more friends.

One of the few great things that came out of me having to move twice in a matter of months: I got really good at remembering to text or call or message people I wanted to spend more time with. It grew out of necessity, but I'm finding that it's almost like a superpower amongst groups of parents. I'd sit here and say that I did something special to get this way, but I didn't. I'm not any less busy than any other person I know; I just started texting people as soon as I started thinking about them. That's it. And even then, I'm not going to pretend to be perfect at it. I just know that it's important that I try.

I know I still have people out there puffing indignantly like: "Well, good for you. Some of us are busy/tired/working/anxious socially." And I have to say: except for that last thing, you're no different than any other parent out there. We're all busy, we're all tired, and we all need to be able to hang with someone who gets what that's like. If you're using that as a reason to not pick up your phone for thirty seconds to send a quick message, you're going to keep being busy and tired all by yourself. I grew up in a time where you had to actually pick up the phone and call people if you wanted to water the tiny seeds of friendship; it takes way less time now, and we should be making the most of that.

Here's the other thing: The joy of texting is that you don't have to answer back right away if your hands are full, or if you're busy. You don't have to reach out to every single person every day, and chances are, of five people you message in one day, two will actually try to get back to you quickly. You're simply exercising effort that every great friendship needs.

Does this mean that everyone will answer back, or put forth the same effort as you do? Nope. Some people are scatterbrained, some won't care about you as much as you care about them, and some will already have friends and won't want any more. The Law of Numbers, though, says that if you make it a habit to reach out to people you like regularly, someone is going to return the favor. Probably more than one someone. In fact, I'd be willing to bet my house that it'll be more someones than if you don't reach out to anyone at all because you're too busy feeling sorry for yourself.

For those of you reading this who have social anxiety, I also get you. Maybe approaching someone on a playground or in a big room isn't your bag, and that's also cool. You know how I met one of my best friends? Digitally, on an app. I let the internet do the work for me.

The app is called Peanut, and it's great. The thing connects you with moms nearby, and you get to "swipe" up or down on people you want to meet or don't want to meet. Sarah, that friend I told you about, was a person I swiped up on. Our first conversation was via message, and I didn't hear her voice until a week after we'd "met." That being said, we still made the effort to meet in person. There was still work involved. And pushing past our personal struggles, whatever they may be, to put forth that work resulted in one my favorite friendships to date.

I also know that many of you out there might just hate how much energy it takes to make and keep mom dates – especially if you're new to an area and going on tons of them over a number of years. I'm not even going to disagree with how awkward those things can be.

Real quick, in case there are any dudes reading this, just so you're up to date on what these things actually are: Mom dates are get-togethers formed by two or more mothers who have decided that they may like to hang out more often. They are named as such because the women are usually on their best behavior, and each probably has their own exit strategy just in case shit gets weird and they have to vacate the premises. Mom dates are often kept short in the beginning, and they're usually something that no one will ever want to actually do again, like eating out at a restaurant with kids in tow or fancy afternoon tea. A lot of probing questions are asked, and at least one person will gently correct their child's behavior to hide that they usually yell. The goal of every mom date is to find a friend –or, if you're lucky, a group of friends – who'll eventually love you even if you launch into a swear-laden tirade about how your kids never pick up after themselves.

I'm fairly certain that dads do not have an equivalent to these. My husband has gone out with a group of other fathers and has come back with absolutely no further knowledge of any of the guys he just spent three hours with. From my understanding, they're all vaguely aware that they each have children, but there is no discussion about them.

Judgment seems to be limited to whether or not the guy is a dick, and…that's kind of it. Maybe it's more than that. I don't know. All I do know is that there isn't anywhere near as much fact-finding going on.

For some, this whole mom date thing is invigorating. It's a way to really get to know women in your community, it's a way to connect with new people, and it's a way to get out of the goddamned house. There's nothing wrong with any of that. I just think they're awful, because regular dating stressed me out. This is not much better.

To those of you who feel judged going to these things, you *are* being judged. You have to be. In fact, you should also be judging. Not to the point of being cruel or exclusionary, but the whole point of these things is to see if you and the other person/people connect on important issues. There's very little real bonding going on during most of these things, because you're mainly trying to make sure that you're not going to wake up one day to another mom or group of moms trying to wear your skin as a hat.

I'm just going to remind you of a very important lesson that many of us forget: you don't owe anyone anything. It's okay not to feel connected to the person you're meeting with, and it's okay not to hang out with them again. We're always taught that rejection can hurt another person's feelings, and that this is bad, but it's possible to reject friendship and to still be nice. I've seen it multiple times, trust me.

I still remember going to a get-together that consisted of a large group of mothers who seemed to know each other pretty well already. As they fed their kids leftover *Duck à l'orange* out of biodegradable bags and commiserated with one another about private schools and the cleaning lady coming on Tuesday, I stuffed a hastily-made PB&J into my son's mouth and stayed mostly silent. As they talked about the magic of watching their children, kids with names like Hunter and Bradley and Smith van Von Smithington the Third, I found myself wishing privately that my son was at a daycare so that I could get a nap. These women were super kind to me; they were very inclusive, they asked me questions, and they even offered my son some of their homemade trail mix. We all knew I didn't fit in that group. We all knew that I didn't have anything to contribute to the conversation, but they were still kind. It serves in my mind as a testament to the fact that an unsuccessful mom date can still be a positive one.

Maybe that'll help your discomfort with the process a little, maybe it won't. I just wanted to make sure you knew that I, too, see mom dates as a necessary evil, and you are not a jerk if you don't like them. Just don't stop doing them, because it's very possible that another mom – the perfect best friend for you – is probably sitting there, hating it as much as you do.

Many of us tend to just wish that we'd run into the people who totally get us. We hope that we'll wander to a park and make eye contact and the other person will just happen to have snacks that our kids like and opinions that we agree with. Even if that happens, we don't like the idea of having to actually follow that up with effort. We don't like that because effort sucks, and it's time-consuming, and if we're low on anything outside of energy, it's time. We don't like doing that because, what if we give our very limited attention and free-time to someone who judges us or makes us feel worse about ourselves? What if we're left feeling even more isolated than before?

These are all valid fears, to be sure, but we need friends just as much as we need medicine when we're sick. They're a form of self-care and self-support. Friends are how we are regularly reminded that we're worth getting to know beyond our kids. There really isn't any other way to continually reconnect with your adult side. I mean…outside of your spouse, if you have one. But it's not fair to them, or to you, to expect your partner to be your only support. We need people who love us outside of a romantic relationship, who don't shit themselves or cry when we suggest things they don't like. If we don't have those people in our lives, we go stir crazy and we forget who we are. So if you have to, look at it like you're putting in the emotional effort for yourself – after all, how's that saying go? "If Mama ain't happy, ain't nobody happy?" I think we know that's true by now.

So take those steps for your happiness. I'm certain you won't regret it.

Labels get in the way. Try to watch how you use them.

Y'all, we're parents. We're literally expending 75% of our energy trying not to choke tiny brain damaged people all day. We're not roving the streets in leather jackets and pulling switchblades on old ladies. So how about we stop acting as if we're competing in some sort of lame-ass gang war that no one wins?

I get that we want to ensure that we're in groups with others who identify with our values. I get that if you're staunchly against fighting, the group of ladies running an underground toddler fighting ring will most likely not be your people. You definitely need to take these things into account. That said, if you're looking your nose down on any one group simply based off of the fact that they're "Pinterest Moms" or "Fitness Moms," you're part of the problem. Simply taking ideas from a website doesn't make a person any more or less of a match for you. Liking kale smoothies denotes a loss of taste buds in a horrible mouth accident, but it doesn't mean they can't be a supportive, worthy friend.

In trying to understand our identities after kids, we've gotten into a rather clique-y mindset towards one another, which wouldn't necessarily be a bad thing if we weren't trying to exclude and avoid, rather than to connect. There's a lot more rolling of eyes at one another than there should be, and I can't help but feel like it has something to do with us feeling like we're looked down upon by society for every fucking thing we do "wrong," which leads to us trying to find someone that we can look down on in turn. Naturally, as the proverbial shit is rolling downhill, you don't want to be the last stop.

The problem with this thinking is, the people who revel in shitting on your parenting aren't seeing any differences between you who lost your kid in the garage once, and Maude, who literally hovers above her kid in an air balloon. You think the same assholes who blame parents for anything and everything are gonna be like "Oh no wait…that's Juliet. She likes Zumba. She's cool?" Not at all. So why play into that? Why not drop the pretense and stop trying to define and reject by hobbies? It's not getting you anywhere, and it definitely can get in the way of you making any real friends.

You can differ in a number of things and still connect on the right issues. I have friends who go to church when I don't, who eat vegan when I love cheese, and who don't drink when I'm thinking about wine at 10 AM (not that I'm drinking it that early. I'm just thinking it might drown out the voices in my head because those voices sound a LOT like my children whining and I don't have the patience). Being a "wine mom" or whatever doesn't make you any better or worse than anyone else. Well, it can make you worse if you use that as a reason not to talk to someone. But otherwise, these descriptors mean precisely dick.

And while we're on this, a side note:

Let's talk about this "hot mess mom"…uh…mess

Pretty sure we all know what a "hot mess mom" is, but in case you're lucky enough to have not heard this descriptor, I'll give a quick definition.

The Hot Mess Mom (henceforth referred to as HMM) is a mother who does not have her shit together always, is very imperfect, probably swears and drinks, loses stuff, and is…well, a hot mess. I hear they're using the term "unicorn mom" now, too, which might mean the same thing? I don't know. The point is, HMMs still care about their kids, but they're fumbling along just like anyone else.

So I'm a hot mess in a lot of ways. We've been through a few, and I'm sure you've caught a few on your own by now. I am far from perfect and I love to be honest about it. Messy hair, dirty houses, and vodka are all my thing. So when I say that I get the draw of videos, articles, and books that revel in being a mess, I do. So hard, I do.

But, fellow hot messes, we need to quit using this as a new way to look down on people who don't parent the same way we do.

You know what I mean. Don't even start looking around all confused like you don't know. It started with honest, noble intentions, because we started out feeling judged and looked-down-upon by the "perfect" moms: the ones who showed up to PTA meetings and made pie and had the wherewithal to say things like "fiddlesticks" in front of their children. We wanted to prove that a good mother can still drink, swear, and chase after their kid at the mall for about five minutes (they just move so *fast*) without automatically being terrible. We wanted people to understand that parents are people who don't have to erase their entire personality to still raise good, intelligent children. It's just that, somewhere along the way, we started using this as another way to divide ourselves instead.

I've seen groups of women sneer at someone who was kind just because they always showed up in Louboutin heels to playdates. I've seen women excluded for feeding their children organic food – not because they were a pain in the ass or pushy about it, but simply because they made it all themselves. I've even heard snide comments made between mom friends because one didn't believe in screen time. No pressure was put on the mom who showed her kids TV; she just felt it was necessary to be snide.

I know where this comes from: it's a defense mechanism, born of years of judgment and condescension over the things we're still not "supposed" to do. Many of my fellow hot messes feel that it's necessary to get out in front of the rejection by rejecting first. Doing that just turns the whole thing into a different side of the same coin, and it makes us look insecure as shit. We should really quit doing it.

"But Arianna," you say, looking down at the stains on your shirt, "you've already made a few jokes in here that sure sound like you're making fun of other moms. You special or something?"

First of all, I make fun of everyone. Where have you been for the last five chapters?

Second of all, you won't see me ever saying that "perfect" moms aren't "real," or that they can fuck off with their "fake perfection," or anything of that nature. People are allowed to show us whatever they want to show us. If they want to only share the good shit with us, they can do that. If they want to share their stretch marks and their life-altering IBS, they're allowed to do that, too. We don't get to dictate the stories they tell us, and we don't get to make a call on whether or not someone else's life is "real" enough for us. We also don't get to bitch about how someone else's life sets up unrealistic expectations for us. Other mothers aren't here for you to feel better or worse about yourself. The quicker you get that, the quicker you can make sure you're making friendship judgements based off of real personality quirks, rather than envy or insecurity.

Besides, you're telling me you don't want to make friends with someone who fresh-bakes shit for her kids all the time? I have one of those friends now (hi, Jen). She gets up at like 4 AM and bakes cookies and cakes and pie. I don't know about you, but a friend who makes pie is going to have a lot of extra pie. Guess who gets that pie? Me. I am not too proud for pie. Or cake. Or any baked goods, really.

I'm just saying: don't make pre-judgments and guesses at a person's character solely off of superficial things, and don't let it stop you from making a friend who might actually have very important things in common with you. That shit was made to divide us from one another, and it's time that stopped.

"Yeah, ok, whatever. I don't need 'mom friends' anyway."

To be completely fair, I feel like I hear this from new moms, or women who've been friends with the same people their entire lives, more than anyone else. I still felt like I needed to mention it because YES, YOU DO.

I'm not in any way saying that you should just give up on your kidless friends. I'm certain they're delightful and entirely worth your time; otherwise, they wouldn't be your friends. They just can't understand what parenting is putting you through to the extent that another parent can.

That sudden breeze was due to countless feathers being ruffled. It happens any time this is uttered anywhere. I still remember having something to this effect posted on Scary Mommy and seeing comments doing everything from calling me "exclusionary" to out and out arguing and saying that childfree friends are the best and that "you don't need mom friends."

Maybe *you* don't, and that's totally cool if you've got an awesome village set up that gives you all that you need. In my experience, though, even those who have a strong circle with many childfree friends sometimes wish they had someone to talk to who understands life with kids. Not just the crazy, funny shit that kids do, but also the really complicated emotions and frustrations that come with parenthood in general. There's nothing wrong with that either. No matter what the argument, this can't be empathized with unless it's truly been experienced. Period, point blank.

I think there are two things at play here, when I'm told that mom friends aren't necessary. For one, I think that the person telling me this has probably fallen for that whole "moms aren't cool" thing I told you about earlier. They've come to believe that being a parent means losing who you are, never having any fun, and talking about poop all the time.

I'm not even gonna lie: some days this is true. More days than I would've ever guessed. It's just not true all the time, and that's the part that doesn't get talked about often. Also, mom groups are known to be hotbeds of yappy, judgy women who have nothing better to do than to argue over whether or not feeding your babies sugar will turn them into the next Ted Bundy. This isn't exactly wrong either, depending on where you hang out. It's just a far-reaching stereotype, and it really depends on who you befriend, which is kind of the point anywhere you go.

The second thing at play here is a fear of being exclusionary. This goes beyond parenthood, but since I'm talking to you, that's what I'm going to focus on.

Listen and listen good: There is nothing rude or mean about saying that a person who is not you doesn't know what it's like to be you. They don't. A person without kids can't know what it's like to have them, regardless of how many nieces and nephews they have or how many plants they water a day. Just like I can't possibly know what it's like to have disposable income in my 30's, or what it's like to date at this particular time in history. This doesn't make anyone invalid or useless in all situations; it only means that they aren't helpful in some situations, and that's totally and completely O-fucking-K. We need to quit acting like everyone's personal experiences apply to every situation. Friends don't have to play every role in order for them to be amazing friends. Different people fill different cups, and that's cool.

My point is that for many of us, we fear saying "I hate my kid today." We're afraid to say it because we're afraid of being judged, and while some of us may be fine with simple non-judgement, most of us really need to hear that we're not the only ones. We need someone who's going to look us in the eye and say "I hate mine, too. Let's hate them together over coffee so we can go back to loving them later." Only those who have been through the same shit you have will be able to say that, and it does so much good for the soul to have it in your life.

Don't knock those mom friends, man. They're your saving grace and your support when you really need to know you're not alone.

That Being Said...

Don't waste your time on people who don't fit you at all, or people who don't deserve it. Don't get so fed up with the whole friend-finding mission that you just keep people around because it's easier. Don't let people into your inner circle before they've earned it. Take the time to get a better understanding of the person you're hanging with. Hang on to your crazy until you're certain you can trust them with it; like I said, treat friend-making like dating. Put on pants, actually care about the state of your house, and keep the dark jokes and swear words mostly to yourself, at least in the beginning. You're trying to figure out whether or not this person will be a good fit for you, and you for them. It's emotionally draining and it's a lot of work, and you're going to be tempted to just accept the first marriage proposal, so to speak, so that you can get it over with.

Don't. The aggravation won't be worth the time and energy you'll think you've saved.

As we're all already aware, our energy is a finite resource. We really don't have a ton of it to just give to anyone who wants it. Think of it as a loaf of bread that you have to feed your family. You get one loaf a day, and you have to give slices to yourself, to your kids, and to your partner. Then you have to feed people you talk to in the store, little old ladies you help across the street, homeless people you give a dollar...whoever. You only get so many slices a day, and once that bread runs out, you have to wait to get more. You wouldn't give a slice to Alice down the street who constantly comments on the state of your house, would you? And you wouldn't waste a bite on Karen, who only seems to come to your house when she wants something from you, right? Hell no, you wouldn't, because you only have so much bread and these two are human dingleberries who can find their own bread elsewhere. That bread has to last you, and there are people around you who are way more deserving of a slice. Sounds correct, doesn't it?

So why the *fuck* should you have to trust Karen with your even-more-precious energy, something you don't even get back? Exactly. You shouldn't. So don't.

And don't misunderstand me here: I'm not telling you to shove her into the street and lock the door behind her. I'm saying you can be honest with yourself, and you can be true to your feelings without feeling like an asshole. We wrongly believe that rejection is rude in and of itself because it might make someone sad, and we need to shake out of that. There's nothing particularly wrong with noping out of a playdate because you're an Atheist and the entire group literally thumps people with Bibles as a hello. You're not wrong for feeling like you won't fit in as the only vegetarian in a group of moms who barbecue full racks of ribs together on the weekends. There are people out there who'll be more appreciative of your time and attention, and even better, who may repay your efforts by shoving a slice of their bread in your mouth as you're shoving a slice of yours in theirs. Frankly, that's much more worth the effort.

Believe me, I've been through the slog. I didn't really want to spend my time setting up meetings and playdates for possibly nothing. I didn't want to have to meet yet another new face that I may wind up wanting to forget in a few minutes. I definitely didn't want to sit across from one woman who chose to tell me that she was racist against people from India as if I'd find that funny. But holding on to my principles and staying open to meeting new people gave me some of the best friends I've ever had.

And if you feel like you've been at it forever, especially if you've moved to a new place, find some solace in the fact that those connections—part of what researchers call Place Attachment—don't generally happen until three to five *years* after the move[6]. And that's if you go out to social things regularly and…I dunno…probably don't have children passing you the plague every two weeks.

If you've been living in your hometown for ages and you still feel lonely, remember that change is still a thing, and that parenthood doesn't stunt growth; in fact, it kind of kicks it into high gear. This is going to end some friendships and start others, sometimes causing multiple cycles of friend groups and connections, until you either die or decide to live in a cave. People get older, learn, forget, and move away. There isn't anything you can do except roll with it and let new friendships come to you. But you do have to let them.

So, as you're sitting in that group you don't feel like you quite fit, or as you're going on what feels like your millionth playdate that you're not exactly excited about, do me a favor and at least think about why you're doing this in the first place. It's not so that you can just find a place to park your butt for a few hours – though that's a decent short-term goal most days – it's so that you can find companionship for yourself, and so someone can find a kickass companion in you. It's so that you have someone to laugh with, to cry with, and to ask possibly-dumb parenting questions who won't laugh at you (much). You need support just as much as anyone else, and so you're rubbing elbows with all these different kinds of people so that you can find *your* people. It will take time, and it won't be easy.

Nothing worth it ever is.

---

[6] Warnick, Melody. "Why You're Miserable After a Move." Psychology Today. 13 Jul 2016. https://www.psychologytoday.com/us/blog/is-where-you-belong/201607/why-youre-miserable-after-move

6

You Say "Selfish" Like it's a Bad Thing

As we are told from the beginning, The Perfect Mother is selfless. She is willing to give up sleep, food, and sanity for her children. She will never complain about being too tired or too hungry or too sad. All of her emotions will come secondary, or even tertiary, to those of her family. She will be made out of a strong, but pleasant straw-like material with a catchy saying on her front. She will make a pleasant *scritch*-ing noise as people wipe their feet on her before entering the house.

Oh wait. Those last two were describing a doormat. Easy mistake to make.

Listen, I've already gone over, both here and in my NYAM writings and on our podcast, about how the whole "selfless-mommy-who-lives-solely-for-others" expectation is fucking weird. I'm going to go over it probably many times after that, too, because it's fucking **weird**. Even weirder is our tendency to give in to it, most times without even meaning to. It's so ingrained in us that we're squirming from guilt the moment we even dare to think anything remotely human.

"I want to shower without being bothered. I just want to not hear their voices for ten seconds." You'll think. Followed by: *"I mean, I love them so much. I just need a shower. I hope they don't hate me for that."*

Firstly, to whom are we even defending our thoughts? Why do we feel like we need to defend them? Are the sanctimommies omniscient now? Can they read minds (Jesus, could you imagine?)? Why do we fear that wishing we were a separate entity for five minutes means we don't love our kids unless we qualify otherwise? Who the hell started the rumor that loving your children couldn't also mean loving yourself? Kicking that person in their gonads has become my number one goal over the last few years.

Secondly, we really need to stop worrying about whether or not caring for ourselves, in little ways or big ones, is selfish. Of course it is. Anyone who tells you that showering isn't selfish, or taking time to yourself isn't selfish is lying to you. It's just the good kind of selfish.

I'm amazed at how few people seem to understand that selfishness alone is neither good nor bad. By its very definition, it's just being concerned with oneself without worrying about others. Don't believe me? Check Merriam-Webster:

Definition of *selfish*

1: concerned excessively or **exclusively with oneself: seeking or concentrating on one's own advantage, pleasure, or well-being without regard for others**

2: arising from concern with one's own welfare or advantage in disregard of others

-a selfish act

See?

"But Arianna," you say, shoving your kid off of your lap for the 90th time, "that's bad. Not caring about other people is bad. You're supposed to have regard for others."

I mean…sometimes, yeah. As much as you can, in fact. But not all the time. That's just unrealistic.

Let me give you an example.

Say you are tired. You probably don't even have to get into character for this one. Say that you've slept a total of four hours in the last two days, and you're officially so exhausted that coffee does absolutely diddly squat. Your body is tingling with how tired you are. I can't stress enough that in this hypothetical, you are running solely on fumes. Also within this hypothetical, your kids are not tired. Or, if they are, they're on that weird shit that kids seem to be on where they're still able to run around like crazy people despite being ridiculously exhausted. Either way, they're up and ready to run you into the ground.

Now, let's say they've decided they actually want to go somewhere today. Say it's the zoo. Their favorite animal is penguins, and they suddenly want with all their little hearts and souls to see them in person for some fucking reason. They're insistent and they're cute and they're looking up at you with eyes that say they'll love you forever if you take them, or at least they'll love you until you refuse to buy them a balloon. But that's in the future and this is now, and now they want you to make memories with them in the form of a penguin-centered zoo trip.

Mommy Law as we understand it would dictate that we're "selfless," that we chug the strongest cold brew we can find, we throw on some clothes, and we deliriously drive these children to the zoo. Or that we do some sort of creative artsy-craftsy crap like make a fake penguin village out of household items and then try to take a nap on the couch while they play. We've been taught that in this situation, their needs always come before ours, and that we're terrible parents if we do anything that isn't "being a mom" first and foremost.

I've got news for you: the moment those little squealing pork roasts came into your life, you started "being a mom." So let's squash that one right now.

And in this hypothetical, despite what we might be told by just about everyone, there is another option: The selfish option. The option that involves telling your children, point-blank, that you're too tired to go to the zoo today, and that you will be doing something largely passive until naptime. In this option, there may be tears and there will be disappointment. You may be called mean and they may tell you they don't like you. This option, however, means these things are hardly your problem. In fact, you're kind of hoping they get so riled up that they misbehave badly enough for you to ground them for the rest of the day so that you can sleep uninterrupted. Maybe you put the TV on all day for them. Maybe you let them eat whatever the hell keeps them quiet. This option only requires that you get sleep so that you can think and make it as an adult until bedtime. It is selfish. It is without regard for your children's feelings, for your spouse's feelings, or for anyone's feelings but your own.

And that's good. Go on, with your selfish self.

You have to think about yourself, and only yourself, sometimes. Sure, you don't want to hurt anyone in the process if you can help it, but if you have to disappoint someone in the interest of being healthy or whole, then it is what it is. Disappointment fades. The zoo and the penguins will still be there. The messy house will still be there (unfortunately). The only difference between that first Mommy Law option and the selfish option is you'll be better prepared to handle the things you have to.

Let's be clear about something, while we're on this: it doesn't have to be life or death either. Like, the options don't have to be "crash into a tree while delirious from tiredness" or "get some sleep." It can be as simple as eating a snack that lifts your spirits and not sharing any with your kid. It can be telling them a certain show is "broken" because you're feeling really downtrodden and hearing the godawful theme song again is not something you can handle that day. You're allowed to take your own feelings into account, and you're allowed to make the selfish choice for yourself sometimes – even when your children are involved.

Oh…and let's talk about guilt.

I guess I can't totally blame our fear of selfishness on the all-encompassing "them," because we're also this way due to our own guilt. You remember guilt, right? It's that little voice in your head that screeches at you every time you laugh when your kid swears in public.

Honestly, some of that unspoken Mommy Law is probably in place because of guilt. Somewhere along the line, we decided that guilt was the ultimate indicator of whether or not something was wrong. If we felt bad for doing it, then it shouldn't have been done. And in most cases, that's actually accurate. I can't wait until my children discover guilt, because then I don't have to tell them that farting on one another's heads is not an acceptable way to voice disagreement. We as a species don't know how to see in grey, though, and so we wind up thinking in absolutes, which is -- and I'll put this as gently as I can – fucking stupid.

Every rule has an exception, including this one. We have to think situationally, and that's including when we feel soul-munching guilt.

Make no mistake: I'm not telling you not to feel guilty. You can't help that. Guilt is a chemical reaction in the brain that you have no more of an ability to shut off than any other emotion. People who tell you not to feel guilty are living in a fantasy world, and they're also lying to you because they feel guilty all the damned time; they can't help it either. I am, however, telling you to examine your guilt instead of just blindly believing it when it tells you that you're human scum.

For example, if you shove your kid in a mud puddle, you should feel bad. If they charge you in a fit of rage and you move out of their way, only for them to trip and fall into said mud puddle, you should not. You undoubtedly would, because you're human and you love the little butthead and their cries will sound sad (after sounding like sweet, sweet justice), but in the end, after thinking about it, you would realize you shouldn't. Of course, Mommy Law would probably dictate that you stand there and let your child kick you because you're their oasis of love and peace or something equally asinine. Mommy Law is wrong. You're not obligated to allow yourself to be abused by anyone, fruit of your loins or not. Suck it, Mommy Law.

And real quick, since this is my book and absolute power has corrupted me, I would like to digress to say that the whole "you're their safe place, so simply hug them and absorb their rage, even if they try to stab you with a fork out of anger" sentiment is largely to blame for the rise in mom guilt and I won't stand for it. No, you do not have to respond to nasty attitudes and uncalled-for punches and mistreatment by singing like a Disney princess and offering them pancakes. That's the dumbest thing I've ever heard. You are naturally going to get angry. You are going to want to scream back. You are going to feel strong rushes of dislike and frustration. You are going to want to disconnect from them physically and/or mentally for a while. This is all natural and fine, and in some cases, the disconnection especially is going to be needed to make sure you don't wind up reacting in ways you'll regret. You're not a shit mom for wanting to be your own safe space when your kid is being a grade-A pain in the ass, and I will scream this until I'm blue in the face at anyone who says otherwise. They can feel safe to unleash on you all they want, but you don't have to absorb shit, besides the ice cream you're going to stuff in your face after telling them to go calm the fuck down somewhere else. Do not let that guilt turn you into a dumping ground for poorly managed emotions. Your job is to guide, to love, and to show them that you're their safe space by not making fun of their outfit choices when they catch an attitude; it is not at all your responsibility to sacrifice your own mental, emotional, or physical wellbeing in favor of your kid feeling better at the end of a bad day.

Anyway.

I know that the outside world isn't exactly stingy with the guilt either. If you let any frustration show where the public can see you, you chance being glared at, or worse, approached. If you mention anything about how hard the whole parenting gig has been for you, you can bet your ass that at some point in your life you'll hear that "you chose to have kids, so you can't complain."

That last thing is especially one of the vilest and most hypocritical things we hear, because it preys on the fear and the discomfort and the responsibility we all seem to feel the moment our child opens their eyes for the first time. It tells us that we're monsters for ever daring to think that this person who we brought into the world is anything but perfect, and that the problem is with us, not them. We're the strange ones for wishing they wouldn't draw on walls. We're the fucks ups for being frustrated that our kid has been waking us up at 3 AM every day for the last week. How dare we? We knew this was coming.

Except we didn't. We couldn't possibly. And the people who say this are generally either a) projecting, because they can't handle their own guilt and their own negative feelings towards their kids; b) holding resentment against their own parents for not handling their frustrations in a constructive way, or c) both. That shit isn't about you. It's about them and their discomfort with the way their expectations and reality disagree.

Unless we're going to say these words to every person who makes a huge life decision, every person who moves to a new city or starts a new relationship or starts a new job, this isn't a valid thing to say to parents at all. Seeing as you're raising literal human beings from scratch, you can't possibly predict what hard shit is coming your way. So please do not entertain this "you asked for it" bullshit for a second. DO NOT let it trip your guilt alarm.

I get that all of this is easier said than done. Even with me saying this, I have the absolute worst time not giving into every guilty thought I have. I have anxiety and Obsessive Compulsive Disorder, so it's like I have the same guilt as everyone else, but it also has a megaphone and stays up all hours of the day. I can't nap even if my husband is caring for our children, because I immediately feel like I'm shirking my responsibilities, especially if they start screaming and crying. So trust me, I'm right there with you. What I've come to realize though, with help from a great counselor and a lot of self-reflection, is that a feeling of responsibility or culpability can be wrong.

Guilt is literally a warning system, nothing more, nothing less. And it's an extension of us, so it is fallible. You don't call the fire department every time your smoke alarm beeps, right? Cool. Then maybe you shouldn't automatically stop what you're doing just because you start to feel a little bad about it. Not without really thinking about it, at least.

I still remember, while shopping at the mall with my family one day, I'd promised my kids candy if they behaved, because bribery is the benchmark of a good parent. This worked out very well for me until my husband decided that he wanted to check out a shoe store directly across from the candy shop. My daughter became caught up in the bright lights and colors of the gummy bears in the window, and she made a beeline for the store, cutting off ridiculous numbers of people in the process.

I darted out and grabbed her as someone almost ran into her, and then I pulled her away. Then I turned around and went back to the candy store because, after wrangling two small kids, I decided I'd earned some sour peach gummy bears. I ate most of them. They were delicious.

Where was I going with this? Oh right.

We went home shortly afterwards, and my husband and I were talking in the kitchen when I received a message on my phone. It was from a woman I had met in person exactly once, over a year before the day in question. In the message, she let me know that it was her my daughter had almost run into, and that she was highly offended that I gave her "a mean look" when she tried to say hello to me. She went on to say that since I didn't recognize her, we clearly had no reason to be connected anymore, and that she would be unfriending me on social media.

My immediate reaction to this message was to feel guilty. I sent her an apology, and then I started mentally replaying the mall trip in my head, trying to figure out exactly when I'd seen someone waving at me. Did I glare at anyone? The only look I remembered having on my face was one of abject panic, because I was certain that my child was going to trip someone up while trying to satisfy her sugar craving. Should I have looked up? Did I look up? What the hell is wrong with me?

Then I came back to my senses and realized that I hadn't, in fact, done anything wrong. I had been busy corralling my children, and I'd failed to recognize someone I didn't even know. That was it. Short of making sure an intense grin was pasted on my face 24 hours a day, I couldn't have done anything differently. That little guilt alarm going off in my head, advising me that I'd hurt someone's feelings and was therefore wrong, was doing its job. I was just also doing *my* job by shutting it off when I realized it was full of shit. I did also block this woman from all contact, because I didn't need the added stress and I can be petty like that.

Your guilt is not the boss of you. It's the other way around. You are the CEO, and your guilt is the over-eager intern who's desperate for your attention. Every moment spent feeling mortified is not a moment to cover your face and apologize.

"Arianna," you say, crossing my name off your Christmas card list, "you sound like a sociopath."

Thank you. I try.

Seriously, though. I'm not pushing for us to ignore one another, nor am I condoning hurting others simply to benefit ourselves. What I'm pushing for is for you, Mom, to give more of a shit about yourself. I'm pushing for you to quit letting people guilt you into things that don't help you or, worse, that hurt you. We're probably the only people out there who are expected by our very nature to just surrender everything that made us human in the name of being "good" at what we do. That only stops when we quit falling for it.

One other thing I want to talk about here, by the way:

If you love to work, work.

For the sake of balls, if you're a mother who loves to work — or even a mother who loves doing something that is not being harassed by kids all day long — stop beating yourself up for it.

It's really popular, I know, for us to catch bullshit for wanting to work, so here, I'll start: I love my job. I love writing, I love making up snarky bullshit to put on the internet, I love talking to people, and I love making marketing plans and social media calendars. If I had the option, I would have my children in a daycare while I sat at my computer and worked all day. In fact, the happiest I've been was when I was working from home while my kids were at daycare. They were challenged all day by teachers and encouraged to play with friends, I was getting to exercise my brain, and then we'd all meet up at the end of the day to eat dinner and snuggle on the couch before bed. This time only lasted for about five months or so, but goddamn it was glorious.

I've already mentioned that I don't have to say this, but I will, because I know people need to hear it: This doesn't mean at all that I don't love my kids or enjoy time hanging out with them. Now, as a stay-at-home-working-from-home-whatever-the-fuck-I-am-mom, I have days where I sit out in the yard in the sunshine, eating yogurt with my kids and thinking that I'm the luckiest person in the world. There are millions of shiny moments with my kids that I'd rather chop off an arm than forget.

That's only half the story for me, though. I love creating. I love getting to make shit up for people to laugh at. My kids can't give me that, and it's unfair of me to expect them to. Just like my friends, or the rest of my family, or anyone in my life, they can't possibly be everything for me, and I can't be everything for them. I like to work, and my kids are no worse off and no less loved.

The same goes for you on all fronts. If you love what you do, as long as you're still making time for your family, you shouldn't even sort of feel bad about it. In fact, you should feel proud of yourself for having something that you enjoy, for satisfying that person who is the foundation for Mom. You're defining yourself by multiple facets, not just motherhood, and you're pushing yourself to develop your other skills. You're treating yourself like a whole-ass person, as it should be.

"O-h-h-h, Arianna, I get it!" You say. "Because then I'm showing my kids how hard work can pay off and that they should pursue their dreams, right?"

I mean…sort of? That, and because you have every right to be a fulfilled, self-actualized human being. Parenthood didn't suddenly take away your need to find joy in things; the only people who argue that fact generally tend to be joyless themselves.

Speaking of, let's talk about self-care.

Yes, it's the quintessential passage talking about self-care.

These days, I know some people get a little twitchy about the term "self-care" because it's become a bit of a cop-out that puts all of the responsibility for your peace of mind on you. This doesn't go over well, because as we know, mothers especially need a little more than just five minutes of reading time a night to re-center. That said, I still like talking about self-care for two reasons:

1.   I personally believe that if you take care of yourself regularly, if you maintenance instead of using self-care as an emergency measure, you'll rarely get to a breaking point where you'll need more than an hour or two a week to decompress, and

2.   "Self-care" can mean so many things, it's like *carte blanche* to coddle yourself for once.

I find a lot of literature aimed at women – mothers especially – seems to be horrible at factoring in that life happens. One thing I'll agree with them on, though, is that we need to cut the shit and admit that self-care is a valid to-do list item that we absolutely have to make time for.

We really don't like doing that, because someone somewhere along the line decided that it would be a good idea to spread a massive lie: If you're not spent, if you're not squeezed dry like a tube of toothpaste at the end of every day, you're not doing motherhood right. If you find time to dress yourself up or take a nap or play games on your phone, you're failing at motherhood and you should be flogged. That's the way things are. At least, that's what we believe they are.

We believe this so hard that we foist these beliefs on one another even. It's so bad that we can't even allow one another that sweet, sweet self-care that we all desperately need.

"Julie had time for a massage?" Someone will say with a sneer. "Must be nice. I wish I had time for a massage. I could get one if I had someone else doing all my parenting for me. Some of us actually have to take care of our kids." If you haven't heard this said about anyone, you're probably the one who said it. If you're not even the one who said it, is your friend group looking for more friends? 'Cause I'm available and I tend to only show up to an event every couple of months. You'll hardly even know I'm there.

To the rest of you who have either said this, heard this, or thought this, I'm not ragging on you. I do want you to realize that you're saying this out of pure envy, and that's not a good look. This kind of thinking is what's messing it up for the rest of us, and I want you to realize that there's no prize out there for whomever has the market cornered on suffering. You're not a better mother because you're more miserable. You are not doing the motherhood thing any better because you're sacrificing every little thing about yourself that you need to survive. That's all a myth.

That whole poisonous way of thinking comes from our obsession with money. We tend to judge a person's worth almost solely by how much money they have to throw at their problems. So if you have a job, especially one that makes bank, you're worthy of prestige and admiration. You're "contributing to society." You're giving of yourself, and you have a quantification of how much that's worth written on regular checks. People can tell you're worth something, and it makes them feel better, because humans are nuts and we have to quantify everything.

You can't quantify motherhood, though. Nobody pays you for it. It can't be measured, and that makes people nervous. So we've been taught over time that the only way you can prove your worth, since it can't be quantified with money, is to give up a much less renewable and only somewhat-measurable resource: your energy. We may not be able to put a number on your worth, but if you're visibly tired and stressed out and tied to your child every time we see you, then we know that you're "worth it." You're doing it "right." On top of "some other smug shit in quotation marks."

This is how we feel obligated to give all of our time and energy to our families. This is why we tend to feel little twinges of guilt if someone sees us on our phones at the playground. Because we can't give cold, hard cash to prove that we're "contributing," so we'd better let them see us give some of—if not all of –our time and energy. It's become the norm, and we're throwing it in each other's faces instead of admitting that it's probably not the best way to decide anyone's worth. We've gotten so bad at this that we even shout how tired we are at total strangers just so that they know what hard-working, loving moms we are.

For example, I saw an article on the internet written by a lady who seemed nice enough, suggesting a number of ways that tired moms would be able to fit in a few moments of self-care in between occurrences in their busy schedules. Some of the things — like brewing a custom "tea of the week"—were a little silly, but most of them were fairly solid suggestions. There were things like putting together a playlist of songs to jam to while you're driving the kids around, or making sure to bring your own snacks when going to playdates.

The comments on this thing were so bitter that I needed gum afterwards. I read snappy comment after snappy comment, doing everything from calling the author a "22-year-old, childless Taylor Swift fan" to flat-out saying that they understood that self-care is a thing, but that they didn't have time to take care of themselves. The overall attitude was mutinous and angry, as if the author had suggested tying their kids to posts in the backyard and lounging around eating bon bons. These suggestions were some of the simplest I'd ever seen, merely requiring that you find little moments during the day to make yourself a bit happier. Heaven forbid.

I'm sure some people are wondering if I'm going to say we have to make time for literally everything under the sun. The answer is no. But self-care and friends – who are, in their own way, a form of self-care – are things we often discard as unimportant because they're for us. There isn't enough time for our own frivolities, we tell ourselves. There just aren't enough hours in the day.

No. False. There are enough hours in the day. We just don't prioritize correctly.

Think about it: Every day has 24 hours in it. Say that you get eight hours of sleep every night, so we'll even knock that down to 16. Say you work, and work is an hour each way. So we take away ten hours. Now you have six free hours a day. Those six hours can be used however you want. Maybe you spend one at dinner with your family and two helping with homework. You spend another 30 minutes putting the kids to bed, and then you find you have a choice. You can clean what needs to be cleaned or you can go to bed early (a great way to take care of yourself, by the way), or you can take a hot bath, or you can veg out on the couch and watch TV. You absolutely have the time to fit yourself in, but you have to feel like you're of importance first.

"But Arianna," you say, hurling your calculator at the wall, "what about all of the household things that I need to finish? I can't go to bed with dirty dishes every night. And I have bills to pay. And trash to take out. And a million other things to do. I can't just decide to sit and watch TV at the end of every day because I feel like it."

OK, so first off? You're the only one saying you can't do that. You can, it's just not ideal for totally understandable reasons. Second off, you don't have to make time every day if your schedule is well and truly packed. You can just allow yourself an extra hour or two a week, or a few minutes here and there, for the special stuff. The extra time – whether you have it one day out of the week or multiple days-- is absolutely yours to spend as you see fit. If you're saying you don't have an extra fifteen minutes to put together a special playlist for yourself, the problem isn't with not having enough hours in a day; it's with you not being so kind as to put yourself first once in a while.

At this point, we've probably all heard at one time or another that "self-care" doesn't have to mean going on a cruise or getting nails done. It's literally just about making sure you care for yourself as much as you care for the rest of the family. And instead of lashing out due to guilt, because admitting we have any free time to care for ourselves is supposedly admitting that we're not taking care of our kids, we should be taking these challenges to care for ourselves seriously. Eat that cookie. Drink that tea. Take that nap. Read that magazine. Call that friend. Wear that sweater. Little things matter. Do whatever the hell you have to in order to recharge your personal battery, because the amount of energy you lose a day isn't indicative of anything besides how many steps you took and maybe your need for better sleep habits.

Fact is, self-care is constant. It isn't just special things here and there so much as it's how you treat yourself day in and day out. It's being aware of when you're not up to doing something minor and allowing yourself to say "no." It's keeping in touch with yourself and recognizing when you've had enough of your kids' shit and separating from the situation, either by going to a nearby room to cry for a few minutes or sending them to their rooms. It's not being afraid to tell someone – anyone, yes even your children – to wait a second before you give any more, because you need to gain some of yourself back before you go into a deficit. It's also realizing that sometimes, people aren't going to be happy with your choices in taking care of yourself, and that's ok. As long as you aren't purposely being a jerk about it, you have to do what's best. And if those people give you a hard time about it, perhaps you have to do a little self-care by leaving them behind and finding people who won't. The concept of self-care isn't meant to pressure you into treating yourself like royalty, so much as it's meant to remind you to treat yourself like a person. Sometimes, people need cruises and massages, and sometimes, they just need to be able to give themselves time on the couch with a box of cookies while the laundry waits patiently until tomorrow.

It's also about *making* the time to do it. Just as you'd make the time to care for your sick kid or to take your dog to the vet. Y'know, like a priority. Because it is one.

If you really must look at it in a way that doesn't make you feel selfish, look at it this way: if you continue to let others just take pieces of you without replenishing, you eventually have nothing left to give besides screaming fits and lots of rage. On the inside, you'll be hollowed out with nothing left to give, and the people you love will bear the brunt of it. Then you'll feel even shittier. So really, you need to take care of *you* for *them*.

It's kind of like when I was in the fourth grade and I had a ruler that said "shatterproof" on it. Dumb nine-year-old me bent the ruler as far as it would go until it snapped in half, with one piece flying to the other side of the room. My teacher stopped her lesson and everyone stared at me. All I could think to say was: "It said it was shatterproof."

To which my teacher replied: "OK, class, quick science lesson: with the right amount of pressure, anything can break."

Anything. Can. Break. Even Mommy.

So allow yourself whatever you need to keep yourself together. Ain't nobody benefiting if pieces of you go flying everywhere.

7

You're Going to Screw Up. Get Used to It.

I'm pretty sure my three-year-old thinks I'm an idiot. Every time she speaks to me, there is about a 50/50 chance that I will not understand what she's trying to tell me the first time. She gets super touchy about this, and our conversations then usually devolve into her repeating herself over and over until I either figure it out or she explodes. I'm sure that, in her little head, I'm a complete simpleton and it makes no sense that I'm in charge of mealtimes and household rules. Sometimes, I'm inclined to agree.

There was one day where this happened, and I was already on edge. I don't remember why. All I do remember is that I was feeling like a caged animal and it wasn't really a good idea to look at me, much less talk to me that day. This is a magical way to feel when you live with small people who don't give a shit about your problems, even on days when you don't really have any. Most people are able to sit alone at their desk as much as they can, or they take a day off, or they try to just avoid people. I am a parent, and therefore can't avoid my children because I hear that's generally frowned upon.

So I just tried to sit very still, like a rabbit hiding in the snow. I clutched my coffee with two hands like it was going to run away from me. My knee bounced rapidly, as if I was going to jump through the roof at any minute.

Then my daughter came up to me, whining. I held up a hand.

"Honey, today is really not the day. What are you whining about?" Even now, I can still hear how sharp my tone was. It was practically a deadly weapon on its own. My husband's balls would have probably shriveled and retreated into his body for safety. My daughter just glared back at me and repeated herself, louder this time:

"I want a flapalfloockin!"

I stared. What? What the fuck is a flapalfloockin? What was she asking me for? Why is this shit so hard? Why don't they come out just knowing words? I don't even like crossword puzzles; why am I having to play a riddle every morning to figure out what my damn kid wants?

I took a deep breath and tried to keep my voice steady. "You...want...a flapalfloockin?"

"Noooo!" She screeched. "A flapalfloockin!"

"A flyswatter?"

"FLAPALFLOOCKIN!"

"A flapjack?"

"FLAPALFLOOCKIN FLAPALFLOOCKIN!"

I want to take a minute here to say that if you are a person who responds to people who don't speak your language by still speaking your language, only louder, I hate you. If you have children, I doubly hate you, because you should know better. I know you've been through this, and that is exactly what this feels like. Having the same unknown word yelled at you multiple times with increasing intensity does nothing but alarm everyone. Act it out, draw a picture, Google it...do something that isn't this, because it sucks and it makes you want to gag the other person with a sock.

Anyway. Back to my story. So there I was, trying horribly to guess what it was my daughter was asking for:

"Flight plans?"

"FLAPALFLOOCKIN!"

"Flesh colored Band-Aid?"

"FLAPAAAALFLOOCKIN!"

Then, it happened: My daughter was done with my shit. Her face scrunched up, her eyes filled with tears, and my last nerve exploded into a thousand pieces. We'd reached our respective boiling points.

"I…wa….want...Flapalfloockin!" My child sobbed.

"I DON'T KNOW WHAT YOU WANT!" I exploded. I stood up, waving my arms as if I was hoping to chase bees of frustration away from my head. "YOU JUST KEEP SAYING THE SAME THING, AND I CAN'T UNDERSTAND WHAT YOU'RE SAYING WHEN YOU CRY. I DON'T HAVE WHAT YOU WANT. *WHAT DO YOU WANT??*"

Understandably, my daughter started to cry harder. I would, too, if a person twice my size started screeching at me at full volume. She was totally impossible to understand at this point, and that built up stress and pressure from before drained away as if I'd pulled a plug. I started to just feel empty and hugely sorry for yelling at my kid. Whining is annoying, sure, but it wasn't her fault I wasn't able to understand her. This was one of those times where I felt like that guilt and shame was right to flood through me.

I won't take you through how I sat her down, calmed her, and finally got out of her what she actually wanted ("strawberries"), but I will tell you that I was reminded of a very important lesson that day. I was reminded of it as I held my daughter and felt her little heartbeat through her shirt. I was reminded of it as I realized that I was why her little heart was beating so fast. I was still thinking about it as she wiped her eyes and cuddled me happily for another five minutes without asking me for a thing.

The lesson is this: Let go of the parent you always thought you would be. That person is an idea, a pipe dream. You won't be that person, because you're going to screw up. Some of it will impress upon your kid, and some of it won't. Whatever the result, it is not something that you can stop from happening.

I hear the sound of a thousand hands flapping in dismay, because it's the number one fear of every parent everywhere, I think. When we're given these tiny people, we want to raise them better than we were raised. We want them to be free of whatever pains and struggles we had when we were kids. We want to give them a childhood without the same fears, or doubts, or mental baggage. Every parent's singular goal is to raise a child who won't write a tell-all book about them someday. We all want to feel like we left the world – and our babies – a little better.

I still believe we will, but this fear of ruining our children is unhelpful. Especially since the things you do will 100% impress upon your kids in both positive *and* negative ways. You are the first model of real-life that they know. That's just how it is.

"But Arianna," you say, sharpening your pitchfork, "that doesn't mean we shouldn't *try* to be the best parents we can to our children. We shouldn't scream at them or scare them or hurt them, because they'll remember and then they'll be broken and it'll be all our faults."

Ok, so first off, you're chatty today and I don't like it. Settle down.

Second off, of course we should try to be the best parents we can be to our children. We just need to redefine that, because right now we take that to mean that we should be perfect. The "best parent that we can be," in our minds, is a parent with infinite patience and a spotless parenting record who never gets tired and always wants to stare lovingly into their children's eyes as they fold laundry. This is ridiculous, because we can never be perfect. We weren't perfect beforehand, and adding a tiny, explosive human being with no understanding of how anything works isn't going to suddenly turn us into perfect people. Setting up the definition of your "best" to be something that you can't do is just asking to be disappointed in yourself. The definition of our best really needs to be: "a parent who loves their kids unconditionally and reminds them that humans fuck up, and that forgiveness and empathy are a thing." Chances are, our kids will wind up with some memory of random mess ups anyway. Because, as I've mentioned, kids' brains are fucking weird.

I remember reading an internet thread once where a person said that they had a memory of standing next to a couch at the age of nine or so. Nothing was happening at the time; they were just standing there and thought to themselves "I will remember this moment standing next to the couch for the rest of my life." Then they did.

You never know what a child's brain will absorb. Trying to figure that out, walking on eggshells and not allowing yourself to make mistakes once in a while, is actually going to hurt both of you more than it'll help. You'll drive yourself bonkers, drive your children bonkers, and you're going to feel even worse if your children exhibit any sort of bad habits or ways of thinking, because you're going to feel like *you* messed up somehow.

"I did all I could to make sure I made them happy and well-adjusted!" You'll cry. "How is it that they still have crippling social anxiety?"

Maybe there was that one time when they were five, where you told them not to touch a lamp at a friend's house because they'd break it and it would make your friend angry. Maybe it was because of the time you denied them a Pop-Tart at the store and they responded by crying and wetting themselves in front of a bunch of people. Maybe some kid at school made fun of their shoes relentlessly for a year and they didn't tell you, because – get this—you won't be the only person to influence and shape their world. Or…how's this for another mindblower…maybe they just developed it. You can't know. Not ahead of time. And spending all of your time trying to predict and prevent is going to drive you crazy.

To be clear, I'm not saying you shouldn't temper your behavior *at all* when dealing with your children -- you shouldn't be asking them to drink shots with you until they're *at least* ten – but I personally believe that fearing every negative feeling your child has is more harmful than helpful. Then you're a mess, your child doesn't know how to deal with your neuroticism so they become a mess, and the next thing you know you're sharing your self-help books with your five-year-old. All you can do is focus on making decisions that seem like the right ones at that moment. Sometimes, this will work in your favor, and sometimes it won't. It's not necessary to worry all day and all night that you'll give your kid some sort of negative habit or negative memory about you, because chances are, you will. And it won't be something you expected.

It's OK for you to fuck up. It's OK for you to make a mistake where your kids can see, and it's OK to own up to it. It's OK to lose your shit sometimes, because you've got a lot on your plate and, try as you might, you're going to hit a wall. Also, kids are fucking infuriating sometimes and I'm inclined to believe that Mother Theresa probably screeched at the children she helped sometimes and then just felt really bad about it afterwards.

"FOR THE LOVE OF JESUS CHRIST WOULD YOU STOP HITTING EACH OTHER? I AM TRYING TO FEED Y – I DON'T CARE IF YOU DON'T LIKE RICE THAT IS WHAT YOU'RE HAVING. THERE ARE STARVING CHILDREN IN...HERE. THERE ARE STARVING CHILDREN HERE – YOU'RE ONE OF THEM...Y'KNOW WHAT, EAT THE GODDAMNED RICE!"

And then she'd go say like 50 Hail Marys or whatever and repent. And now she's a dyed-in-the-wool saint. You. Can. Make. Mistakes. And yes, they may affect things in a way you weren't expecting. You know how you can best handle that? By accepting it.

It's simple really: show your kids how a human being – not a TV mom or a Norman Rockwell caricature of an apple pie mom – handles their mistakes. Show them how an imperfect person recovers from anger. As a pretty imperfect person myself, I've found, through conversations with expert friends and fucking up a few times in the past, that there's a pretty decent recipe out there for recovering gracefully when you can. Some of this I learned on my own, and some I learned by reading awesome books (quick plug for the Carla Naumburg, PhD's *How to Stop Losing Your Sh*t with Your Kids*, which is guaranteed to teach you some very important facts about this very subject). So basically, you start with these three things:

Apologize

We're better at the whole apologizing-to-our kids thing these days, but there's still a pretty healthy-sized group of people out there who think that apologizing to your children shows weakness. It's an unhealthy way to think, and I'm glad it's on its way out. So I'm going to try to help that along.

Here's the deal: someday, there's a good chance that your kid is going to have a kid of their own, and your grandchild is going to be a pain in the ass. And that pain in the ass grandchild, plus a random bad day, will become too much to the point where there's yelling. Maybe your kid will even remember how you yelled and how it hurt their feelings. After that, though, they're either going to remember how you immediately ran away to cry and then never spoke of it again, or they're going to remember how you sucked it up, sat them down, and apologized for losing your cool. And then they're going to remember how that helped ease the sting a little. And then they're going to apologize to your grandchild, the way your actions taught them to. The power of a heartfelt "I'm so sorry. I shouldn't have done that, and I love you" is vastly underrated.

Verbalize your feelings

We are *terrified* of letting our children know we have actual feelings. I don't know if this is another fear of seeming weak or what, but we never seem to be allowed to tell our kids how we feel about things. We're encouraged to help them figure out *their* emotions, and to help them verbalize where they're at emotionally, but I have yet to hear someone say the same to parents who didn't sound like the famous part of a cuckoo clock.

Listen, I'm not saying that you have to sit there, trying to have a PhD-level conversation with your kid as they scream in your face at the top of their lungs. That would be dumb, as angry children don't have room in their brains for anything but rage and you will be wasting your breath. However, after the dust has settled, after they are released from their room or after your throat has stopped hurting from yelling or after you've hugged it out and apologized, it's cool to tell them where it all came from. You don't even have to blame your behavior on theirs; it's just helpful for them to know where your head was at when shit went down.

The day I yelled at my daughter like a crazy person, I said: "Mommy's sorry she yelled. She's having a really hard day and she couldn't really understand what you wanted."

To which my daughter replied: "You weren't very nice."

Did I mention that this could also teach your children to verbalize *their* feelings? It could. And sometimes –most times – it'll make you feel worse for a bit. It's all worth it, though, when you know that someday they'll be able to speak for themselves. At least, after their teen years, it will be great.

Oh, and don't be afraid to be honest about how you're feeling when your kid actually *is* the asshole in this situation. I feel like we're never told to do this, because we can hurt our kids' self-esteem or some such crap, but as with everything, it's all in how you do it. If you're all, "Why do you have to be such an asshole? I should've left you in a ditch!" Then yeah, I would imagine that might cause some issues. I'm not saying you have to do that, though.

I figured this out when my son was in a mood one day. He was doing what toddlers do – y'know, destroying shit and annoying people – but he was doing it with an extra bit of enthusiasm that I know he didn't get from me. He was really giving this his all, like 110%, angering both me and his sister every few minutes with some new shenanigans. By the end of it, I was miffed enough that I sent him to his room for some "time to cool down." More for me than for him, but I didn't mention that.

When he came back downstairs, he had a look on his face like he'd been pacing his room, acting out the argument we were going to have. He'd clearly been practicing how we were going to go toe-to-toe with well-placed barbs, only for him to deliver a crushing blow at the end that would teach me what a *bad, bad mommy* I am. His little eyes were squinted and his fists were at his sides. If looks could kill, this one wouldn't have exactly tickled.

"You don't look as if you've calmed." I said.

"You're *mean!*" He retorted. "You're a mean mommy and I don't like you!"

I remember it came out of my mouth before I even had a second to think about it: "Well, you haven't been very nice to anyone all morning, so that's OK. I don't like you very much right now either."

My son looked shocked. Clearly I hadn't said this during any of his fight rehearsals, and he wasn't sure how to respond. I took the opportunity to keep talking.

"I love you and I will always love you." I said. "But when you're mean, I don't like you, just like you don't like me. So maybe you should go back to your room until we can like each other again."

Surprisingly, the kid didn't argue. He just walked upstairs and stayed there. During that time, I had the thoughts all parents do any time they do anything that suggests they're even remotely human:

Great. There goes the opener for his Netflix serial killer special. I shouldn't have said that. Now he's going to hate me forever. I ruined him. I messed him up.

Who knows? Maybe I did. Even though my son returned downstairs much calmer the second time, even though he apologized and came in for a hug, maybe I set him on a more destructive path by telling him how his actions made me feel. Maybe we're not supposed to tell our kids when they're assholes and how that affects the people around them.

I don't at all believe that's the case, but I'm trying to pretend I might because that's what people are probably expecting me to do.

Real talk: I don't think it's wrong for us to let our children know that, in a tense situation, they were not the only ones feeling tense. I think it's good for them to understand that a) douchery won't make them any friends, and b) Mommy is not a robot, as cool as that would be. Mommy has feelings, Mommy gets mad, and that matters just as much as it does for anyone else. The only way they're going to learn that is if you teach it to them.

Anyway. That's when *they* screw up. I'm talking about when we do.

Tell them how the situation made you feel, and then if you didn't react the way that you should have, own up to that. Then, you do the last thing:

Forgive yourself. Fix it.

"But Arianna," you say, rolling your eyes so far back that they get stuck for a second, "the title for this section is two things."

Yeah, but they go hand-in-hand. Also I'm writing this, so I win. Moving on:

Recently, I realized my son might have anger issues. I'm not sure what gave it away. It might have been the first time I saw that familiar gleam in his eye during an argument with his sister. It could have been that time where he Hulked-out on my arm. It could also be that I recognize it, because I used to have the same problems with rage when I was his age. I, too, used to cross a line emotionally that I couldn't seem to cross back over, and it took me until my mid-teens to really learn to control it. Now, I get to watch it from the outside and wonder time and again whether or not his anger problems are *my* fault. Whee.

I've been through many moments of crisis over this. I've wondered whether or not this is because I panicked and tried disciplining him with spanking when he was two. I've wondered if I did this to him by raising my voice too many times. I can't tell you how many times I've sat and pondered whether or not I've ruined his adulthood with the mistakes I've made, how many times I've wondered if he's going to grow up to be a total asshole because of me. Not the fun kind of asshole, either; like the all-caps, grade-A ASSHOLE type. I worry constantly that I've done this to him, because I haven't been able to keep my cool all the time, and hug him even when he's being a total jerk, and be more crafty and make...I don't know...cotton ball sheep? Is that a craft?

Anyway.

Going down this rabbit hole helps no one. It is totally possible that my yelling, mixed with his particular personality, has led to temper issues of his own. I *have* realized, however, that time travel still isn't a thing (yet. I'm holding out hope.), and that it's more important for me to at least try to fix the mistakes I've made, and to move forward towards a positive result, rather than angsting over the past.

Does this mean that I'll never yell again, that I'll completely change my attitude, and that I'll start calling my children "little muffins" or some shit? No. It doesn't mean that I have to change myself at my core; if I'm not the fluffy, sweet kind of mom who turns the other cheek when my kid slaps me, that doesn't have to change. And in case you haven't been listening, there's absolutely nothing wrong with hitting a metaphorical wall, because *something* has got to be there to tell you to slow down. So no, I'm not talking about completely overhauling your entire personality.

I *am* saying that I recognize my faults and I *try actively* to correct them, and if I slip up, I apologize. If I feel that a lesson is in order, sometimes I'll even throw in a big disclaimer that Mommy is a moron, that she makes mistakes, and that you should do as she says, not as she does. And, seeing how my son has started apologizing when he's wrong and taking deep breaths to calm himself down, I'm figuring I must have a point in here *some*where.

All I'm saying is, there's nothing wrong at all with aiming for a great parenting career. You can aim to be loving, you can aim for good memories, and you an even aim to be a "great" mom. You're setting yourself up for disappointment, though, if you aim to be perfect. The moment that you stop trying to control the mistakes you've made in the past and the memories they may have of you in the future, when you've decided just to throw your all into the present, that's when you'll give them the mom you want to give them. That's when kids will get to see that it's possible for a human being with flaws and opinions to love them fully --even if they may not like them for a bit-- and that it doesn't take a super-patient mom-deity to do so.

That's parenthood: Everyone is learning by doing, including you.

8

Your Arms are Too Short to Box with Parenthood

Recently—as in the day before I started this chapter recently—I started potty training our daughter for the third time.

Time number one was sort of a fun little lark, like a "let's just see what happens" thing, because she'd started asking to sit on the toilet like her brother. She quickly got bored with playing around, and she was back in diapers without much fuss from us. Time number two was a one day thing where we hoped that maybe she was readier than before, and it lasted one day, because she was barely two and none of us cared enough to go through screaming and fighting when she asked for a diaper.

This time is the first time we've ever been really serious about making it work, or at least trying for longer than a day. I'm going to be completely honest here: this is happening mainly because my daughter shits like an adult, multiple times a day, and I'm over it. The three-year-old is not the one who should be making the biggest turds in the house, and yet here we are. It's like some lame-o superpower, and I'm not down for being the sidekick.

Anyway.

We started yesterday, and it's proven to be the perfect reminder of how powerless and out-of-control parenting really is. I can't control when she pees – obviously, or our kitchen floor would have been saved some trauma. I can't control whether or not she even wants to go to the toilet. I definitely can't control whether or not she's actually ready for this. She might not be, and then I'm back to carrying monster shits out to the trashcan four times a day. I may be the loudest, the most on schedule, and the tallest person involved in this struggle, but I am absolutely, 100-percent, *not* the one in control here. I am at the mercy of a person who can't even reach most kitchen counters.

That's every parent, everywhere, and it especially falls on mothers nine times out of ten. The moment your kid enters the world, you aren't in control of anything anymore, which would be fine if this was in a big, existential, metaphysical sense. It's a lot fucking harder when we're saying this in a tangible, non-metaphorical way. Your schedule, your health, your mind…it all magically becomes your kids' to mold and shape as they like. Not a morning person? Nobody fucking cares. Sweet Emily can only wake at five AM and she's gonna want breakfast. Hardly ever get sick? Well, Jason just started school and he's licked all the desks. Hope you like barf. Ah, I see you like your breasts as they are: nice and perky and ready to greet the world. Well, you had twins, so I hope you're also a fan of them when they're floppy and sad and constantly avoiding eye contact.

Suddenly, we're not *us* anymore – not to the kids, or the public, or our friends. It's not exactly surprising that we'd feel that way about ourselves eventually. They even did a study on it -- "they" being a team of Norwegian researchers led by guaranteed-Scrabble-win, Weibke Bleidorn – and found that "self- esteem decreased during pregnancy, increased [after birth] until the child was six months old and then gradually decreased over following years," with "mothers of three-year-olds [hitting] a low point in their self-esteem[7]."

So basically, we don't feel so great about ourselves when we're waddling everywhere, being touched by random strangers, and getting winded trying to lift ice cream to our mouths. Then we feel better about ourselves for a while despite the giant cotton pads on our vaginas and the leaky boobs, because we know we made something pretty amazing. If we're lucky, people are bringing us food and playing with the baby, and we're getting attention and bonding with a tiny person that we made, and all is well. Then we start realizing that we're never going to sleep in again, that this tiny, screamy thing is *still* pretty screamy, only now they're cutting teeth, so it's worse. We also start to notice at six months that we're kind of this little screamy thing's bitch. There's something dehumanizing about that, about knowing that if your kid pulls down your shirt in public or screams at you or humiliates you, you're not allowed to react with anything but calm and sweetness. Or a stern talking-to and a time out. You won't really know what the right answer is, but you will notice that everyone is watching you and judging your parenting. So there's that. There's also the fact that our bodies don't always "snap back" the way we were told. And our boobs might still be leaking. And then we have three-year-olds, and all of our hope for appreciation goes to shit when the kid thanks you for your dedication by telling you that your new haircut makes you look like Elmo.

And the worst part is, nobody cares or even expects more from you, because you're a mom now. Moms are naturally gross, perpetually-tired automatons who'll answer every scheduling question with "Let me check to make sure my kids aren't doing anything that day." Nothing is yours anymore. Doctor appointments and meetings and important engagements are regularly rescheduled in favor of games and meetings

---

[7] Bleidorn, Wiebke, et al. Stability and Change in Self-Esteem During the Transition to Parenthood. *Social Psychological and Personality Science.* 29 Apr 2016.

and sickness. Every drawer or closet or closed door is but a futile attempt at maintaining privacy, which you definitely don't have anymore – the tiny tyrant dumping flour on your floors has seen to that.

When you aren't running your own ship anymore, and when no one else expects you to, it's easy to lose hold of yourself, and to just stop expecting much of yourself and life in general. Understandably, this also makes you super grouchy.

"But Arianna," you say, probably checking your own hair to make sure you do not, in fact, look like Elmo, "I can tell you right now that Lisa down the street is *totally* in control. She runs her own business, and she's on the PTA, and her husband cooks her all of her favorite meals, and she makes sure her three children *never miss a soccer game.* She doesn't have to kick her nipples out of the way when she walks, and she owns a brand new mountain bike. She is definitely in control of her household, and I want to be more like her."

Ok, so first off: I feel like we've been over this. Stop trying to use Lisa as your personal barometer for life. Lisa has abilities and inabilities and privileges and problems that you probably don't know about. Lisa is doing Lisa. Let her live.

Second off: Lisa isn't in control of a damn thing except maybe her bowel movements, and she has three kids so even that's questionable. What Lisa has done is take control of what she can. Instead of allowing herself to feel helpless, she tries to steer as much as she can in directions she can handle. We actually *all* do that, to a degree. We try to compensate for our sudden loss of autonomy by trying to control as much of our lives as humanly possible, and some of us (like me, for example), do little petty things like buy stupid coffee mugs for an ever-growing collection that inevitably throws our spouse into a rant about running out of cabinet space. We try to take some control out of a situation wherein we have very little.

If you think I'm going to tell you to stop doing that, you're out of your mind. I think you should keep it up.

Truth is, we change a *lot* after children. We have no choice. I know I spend a lot of time with NYAM talking about all of the things that don't change after children, and I do that because I feel we could use the reminder. We're all actually well aware of what's changed. We struggle, though, with reconciling that in our heads. Keeping hold of the things I can control is definitely one of the more helpful things in my personal toolkit.

Here are a few others, in case you're feeling frisky:

Remembering that motherhood doesn't automatically mean constant, unending sacrifice

Ah yes. The almighty "sacrifice" that serves as the gold star we give ourselves at the end of a long day. It's our favorite word to throw out when we want to sound brave and loving and compassionate, despite actually being pissed that we had to give something up. We've been made to feel as if "good moms" give away, and that "bad moms" hold tight. Parenthood is like being in a monastery; only the humblest and poorest and quietest are the ones who attain enlightenment. It's gotten so bad that we can't even look at ol' Lisa down the street with her store-bought breasts and her brand new mountain bike without seething.

Listen here, friend: Lisa is celebrating herself. She's living her best life, as best as she can, because she's the only one who will focus on it every day. Her kids don't give a shit about her happiness and have the attention span of goldfish. Her partner works long hours. That's not to say that her family doesn't remember to value her on occasion, but the only person who is going to appreciate Lisa constantly, without fail, is Lisa. She's realized this, and she's doing something about it.

Motherhood *includes* sacrifice. It doesn't *equal* sacrifice. The quicker we get that through our heads, the better.

Sure, you are going to have to sacrifice sleep. You are going to have to sacrifice time. Taking care of tiny people with no survival instinct will absolutely call for you to stand down on things you want or need sometimes, especially as a mother, because whether you stay at home with the children or work in an office, it's pretty widely accepted that this is your "job" now.

You do *not* have to sacrifice happiness, or friends, or comfort though. Not every time, anyway. You have the right to spend money on yourself sometimes, if you've got it. It's totally cool for you to take naps whenever you can, because sleep is fucking awesome and countless studies have shown that we don't get anywhere near enough of it. You are allowed to be unhappy that you have to do something you don't particularly want to do, even if it's for your children.

Be honest about your feelings, wants, and needs. It's a fantastic way to keep in touch with who you are, and to keep hold of the little parts of you that you actually *don't* want to lose.

This is also why it's important to hold on to your favorite pre-kid hobbies. If you didn't have hobbies, it's important that you try to find one.

"But Arianna," you say, sniffing your child while their back is turned, "my *child* is my hobby."

Where is my spray bottle? NO. **NO**. **Bad**.

Child or not, a person is not a hobby. You should never tie your feelings of enjoyment and fun to any one person, because you're asking for trouble – especially when that person is someone who'll (hopefully) eventually grow up and move out. You can love your child with all of your heart and think the sun shines out of their ass, but I'm advising *strongly* against doing absolutely nothing for yourself. Not only can that lead to a complete loss of yourself and what that means, but it also leaves you absolutely no chance to exercise the parts of your brain that aren't blown out by child-rearing. It doesn't even have to be anything extravagant; get into puzzles, or knitting, or reading. Make sure you enjoy it enough to feel some relaxation and joy when you do it. Holding on to that will ensure that you don't feel like you've lost your hold on all parts of you.

On the other side of this coin, the second thing I'd suggest to help you with these crazy-ass changes is this:

Admit that you've changed a bit

I know a ton of people who feel that it's more empowering to say that they haven't changed at all since becoming a parent, but I disagree. It just depends on *which* changes you decide to focus on.

I, for example, was even more of a hot mess before becoming a parent. Sure, I only had to worry about myself and I was rocking a decent grad school career, but I wasn't driven and I didn't think things through. After kids, I am far from perfect, but I'll be damned if I don't have more of a laser focus. Some of it is because I want to set a good example for my children, and some of it is that I know I only have, like, two hours a day to get shit done without someone demanding something from me. Whatever the reason, I'm better at getting things done now that I'm a parent. That's a change I don't mind embracing, and it's one I'd gladly credit to motherhood.

Focusing on the good changes you've been through helps to keep you from feeling like life has just shifted on you without you having any say-so. It also helps you to keep from locking your kids outside when they're being particularly annoying. After all, without them, you wouldn't be stronger or more patient or more driven. Their need for your guidance changes you in some of the best ways possible, and that is something that helps to underline how parenthood serves as an evolution, not a full-on phase shift.

And while we're on the subject, I think it's time that some of us stop fighting parenthood. You know how I mentioned those people who deny the importance of mom friends? The ones who think that mom friends are a gateway drug to becoming an uncool stereotype? I don't totally blame them, because this whole parenting gig has a really shitty PR team. Somehow, we've gotten into this place where the "cool" parents – that is, the ones who are socially acceptable and "fun" – are the ones who don't "act like" parents. They come to parties and get-togethers all the time, they put all work and extracurriculars first, and they would *never, ever, ever* think to visit their children's behavior on others. This includes totally normal kid behaviors, like crying or laughing or getting antsy. These people snap at their children for getting bored after an hour at a childless friend's house full of shit they can't touch, and look down their noses at parents whose kids cry in restaurants.

Stop it. You don't have to pretend you aren't a parent to be "socially acceptable." You don't have to prove you're cool by talking endless shit about your kids. You can be a parent and be a really cool human being; stop letting people pressure you into proving you're "not like those other parents."

"But Arianna," you say, taking a very confused glance at the book cover, "don't you run a project called The Not Your Average Mom Project? And you talk shit about your children endlessly."

Listen: My point is that there *is* no average mom. I've talked to teachers, sex workers, business owners, and many others who share average motherhood *moments*, but who couldn't be any more unique if they tried. None of us are your average mom, because an "average" suggests sameness, and we're all still such different characters with colorful stories that it blows my mind sometimes how we still believe that a kid or seven can ever erase that.

And as far as talking shit about my kids goes: I mean, I don't do it to seem cool. I just do it because it's funny and I'm certain they're going to do the same to me one day very soon. They are my kids, after all. If you think it's cool though, I'm flattered.

The moment that you realize that parenthood –like any other major life change— leads to growth, you don't have to be afraid of admitting that there are parts of you that have changed. The pressure drops, and then you're able to just enjoy the actually enjoyable parts of parenthood.

Oh, and this helps, too:

Don't expect to be thanked.

My daughter woke up vomiting late one night, fairly soon after our Costa Rica trip. It was past midnight, and it was gnarly. My husband was the one to stumble upon it, and I was the one dumb enough to offer to help clean it up. Strangely, I was able to push any anxiety or disgust down long enough to gather up ruined sheets and shove all yak-covered stuffies into the washing machine. Somehow, I even found it in me to make sure that my husband positioned my daughter over the toilet just in time for her to throw up again.

After all this excitement, we were sitting next to each other on the edge of the tub as our daughter played, waiting to see if there was going to be another vom-wave. It was about 1:45 AM or so, and we both had to work in the morning. I had to drive an hour away to start at 7 AM. As I started wondering whether or not sleeping at red lights is illegal, my husband turned blearily to me and said, without an ounce of irony: "I'm tired."

There are moments in relationships where we reach a crossroads. In this particular moment, I had the option of either responding to his sentence with kindness and empathy, or being like: "OH REALLY? YOU'RE TIRED? NOT ME, BITCH, I'M READY TO RUN A 5K." I chose the first thing, and offered to stay up with our daughter while he went back to bed.

After another fifteen minutes, I decided our daughter was good to lie back down, and I set her up in her crib on a towel, then covered her with another towel. As I'm tucking her in, she looks up at me, panicked. "Where's Yaya?"

I cringed. Yaya is this tiny, dirty giraffe toy that she carries everywhere. It was in the pile of things I'd had to shove in the wash. I told her so, and she started to cry. I felt for her; I don't know anyone who wouldn't want comfort when they've been up vomiting all night after almost a month on and off of battling a stomach virus. So I promised her I'd bring Yaya to her when he was done drying. I swore he'd be next to her when she woke up the following morning. That was the only thing that would get her to sleep.

I stayed up, listening for the dryer and for any more emergencies, until 3:30 AM. As soon as the dryer buzzer went off, I retrieved the stupid giraffe and tucked him in next to my daughter. Then I went to bed and tried to sleep until I had to get up for work at 6 AM.

I spent the next day at work bleary, but also kind of relieved that I wouldn't have to clean up anymore vomit. Neither did my husband, apparently, because she was completely fine the entire day. But no matter; I decided that when I got home I'd hold my baby, and that she would thankfully nuzzle into my shoulder with Yaya, and touching music would play and my crazy night would all be worth it.

Except, when I got home and opened my arms for a hug, my daughter screeched "DON'T TOUCH ME! I WANT DADDY!" and ran away from me. So...nope.

That was okay, though, because I turned to my husband with open arms, waiting for a hug and a "thank you for taking over last night so I could get sleep." I got a hug. I did not get the second thing. To be fair to him, he cared for our daughter all day while I was at work, but I would be lying if I didn't admit I was a little miffed.

Let's be clear about something here: there is absolutely *nothing* wrong or weird about wanting to be appreciated or thanked for doing hard shit, even if it's a regular part of parenting. People expect it every day in the form of paychecks or an actual, spoken "thank you." It *is* really fucking weird and wrong that we're told that we can't want that simply because the hard shit was in the name of helping our kid. Of *course* we're allowed to want someone to thank us for being tired or giving up food or canceling plans. We just also have to realize we're often not going to get it. Once we come to terms with that, and the fact that we can't really control whether or not people see and appreciate what we do behind the scenes, it'll make things a little easier.

Like, hell no, I'm not going to tell you not to say something if you feel like you're being taken for granted. If you're never eating hot meals because you're cooking for and serving everyone else or if you're never getting sleep or time to yourself because no one is listening to your cries for help, then by all means cry louder.

That said, we've crossed into a strange land. Before we had children, it was totally understandable to want or need acknowledgment for the things we did. After they entered our lives, struggling became our job, so any time that we're tired or ready to snap or covered in someone else's bodily fluids, it's something we're just expected to go through. And we will do it without complaint, and we will do it expecting no repayment but the love of our children, depending on their mood. While this is utterly insane and not at all how anything works, there is a little bit of a point there, because life is full of inconveniences, and we can't be thanked for every single one of them.

Trust me, I've been there: I've had moments myself where I've gotten mad when I've been asked to do something massively inconvenient, because I know it'll never be acknowledged or thought of twice, and I know that people will just say something cutesy like "welcome to motherhood." Because the day I laid in labor for 34 hours wasn't welcome enough.

That said, once we make peace with the fact that a lot of those inconveniences won't be recognized, we can do two things. We can:

1.   Stop feeling like we're just living around the lives of literally everyone else, and

2.   Celebrate our damn selves.

Number one probably sounds a little counterintuitive, but stick with me here. Once you become aware that you'll probably be driving little Bobby to his soccer practice while sick with a nasty cold and drained of all energy without so much as a "thank you," you'll free yourself from the tether that comes with high hopes for recognition. Think about it: when you're wishing someone would just give you a cupcake and a nap, you're stabbed in the heart with disappointment when it doesn't happen. That disappointment is inevitably followed by resentment and anger and feelings of hopelessness. You're suddenly like "Why did I even do this if no one is going to be thankful I did it?" And then you're side eying your kids and thinking of going on strike.

On the flip side of that, if you tell yourself before you climb into your car to take Bobby to practice that you're just going to do this because it has to be done, the situation becomes something you're doing under your own power rather than anyone else's. You're aware that you can't control whether or not anyone realizes what you've done, but you *can* control whether or not *you* realize it. And then you feel a little pride in yourself, and then you make the decision whether or not to yell "YOU'RE WELCOME!" as your kid jumps out of the car. Maybe you will, maybe you won't. But now, you're doing it because it's connected to your own sense of duty, not because you're hoping that someone will notice what a bomb-ass mom you are.

That part comes with item number two. See, after you get Bobby home, now that you're already aware of the fact that you're a bomb-ass mom and that you're not obligated to be sick and miserable to prove it, you can sit Bobby down with cereal for dinner and lie down on the couch. You can tell yourself "they don't have to thank me, but I'm going to thank *myself* by taking care of my health. I'm going to down some nighttime cough medicine, and I'm going to bed." Or maybe you point at your spouse, then your kid, and head upstairs to bed. Or maybe you just down three ice cream sandwiches and cry under the table until everyone else goes to bed. Whatever feels like a reward for you, you do it. Not because anyone else in your family verified that you deserved it, but because you already knew that you did.

Remember when I said that it's *really* important that we hold on to the things we can control? This is what I meant. By making sure you thank yourself sometimes, you're removing some of that power that any outside gratitude (or lack thereof) holds over you. You're allowing yourself to decide on the actions that make you a bomb ass mom, rather than letting thank yous decide.

You know what this is like? It's like this one time I was at the grocery store and my kids insisted on "helping" me push the cart. They sucked at it, and if I'd left them to their own devices, the cart would've gone careening into everything in our path. So I, with the upper body strength of a gerbil, tightened my grip and kept the cart rolling straight as my children squealed with glee. Finally, one of them looked up at me and said: "Mommy, look! We're doing it! We're pushing the cart!"

Obviously they weren't doing it, and I could have set them straight. I realized though that this wasn't really a battle worth fighting. It wasn't worth the breath to point out that I was keeping us on course. I knew the truth; it didn't really matter whether they did or not. So I just kept pushing us forward and putting groceries in the cart, all the while thanking the powers that be for the arm workout. That's why I'm trying to get you to celebrate yourself – so that even if it seems that no one notices that you're keeping everything going, at least sometimes, you're able to push ahead and keep filling your own cup. Or cart, as the case may be.

You certainly deserve thanks and appreciation and acknowledgment for the things you do. Without a doubt, you do. I just don't want you to entrust all of the gratitude to others. I want you to be able to handle some of that shit yourself. Living that way leaves you happier, it makes you more likely to ask for things you need, and it helps you to be able to pick your battles so that you only lend your energy and focus to the moments that actually call for it. I still have days where I fail miserably at this, and I think it's human nature to fail miserably at this on a bad day, but I want you to still try. I want your family to learn your boundaries and your triumphs, and I want them to notice them, but I want you to show them *how* to do that. If you're lucky, they may even catch on pretty quickly.

If you take nothing else away from this chapter, I want you to take this: suffering is no one's job. I will repeat until I'm dead that it's a part of life, but it isn't a badge of honor or proof positive that you're somehow nobler than the woman who makes sure to take a personal vacation twice a year. You know how we're told to "cherish those little moments" with our families? Your own personal "little moments" need to be cherished, too, and your own funny sayings and idiosyncrasies and joys should also be celebrated by those you love. That doesn't go away because you're a mother. And if you have to head the campaign to make sure that this happens, I'm telling you that you absolutely can without sacrificing your value as a "good mom."

"But Arianna," you say, shaking your head so hard you damage some of your memories, "parenting *is* a thankless job. That's what it's supposed to be. What do you want, a parade every time you wash the dishes?"

That would be nice, actually. How quickly do you think we can get a float of my face made?

In all seriousness, I'm not saying that these things will stop you from feeling unappreciated or tired. Parenthood lasts way too long and involves way too many variables for you to ever perfect anything. You'll still wind up making sacrifices, people will still fail to notice, and you're still going to want them to. Most days, it will still be on you to support your family in as many ways as necessary to help those assholes succeed. You just also need to remember that you need support and encouragement to succeed, too – whatever that may look like.

The moment that you accept that parenthood is about you, too, you realize that you're in control of so much more than you're often led to believe. Then being covered in shit or staying up until the wee hours of the morning to deliver a clean stuffed animal seem less like evidence that you're someone else's robot, and more like actions a human willingly does when they love another human.

You get your *love* back. Both for yourself, and for the new life that you've grown into. No matter what, once it's yours, the entire world can't take that from you.

9

You're Not Wonder Woman. Wonder Woman is a Fictional Character

I'm just gonna cut right to my thesis here, people: Quit trying to be a superhero.

I know there are a million articles and books out there that say otherwise, and T-shirts with cutesy little sayings on them like "I'm a Mommy, what's your superpower?" I know I probably sound like a dick right now because you're wearing that shirt as you read this. I know that you want to argue that we do all of these things that no one else does, and we're often not appreciated for it. I know you're probably sick of me ruining things and you'd love it if I'd just let you live. But I need you to hear me out, because our constant need to be "super" at every little thing is part of the problem.

I've already mentioned how the rest of the world wants us to be a million things at once, so I won't really go into that again. Now I'm starting in on *you* and how you fell for that shit so hard that you expect *yourself* to be a million things at once. In fact, you find pride in it. When you're able to tell people that you "have hustle," or when you tell people you're "busy," it makes you feel accomplished. You literally *love* it when people say "I don't know how you do it. That's so much! I wish I could get that much done in a day." In fact, any time that you have to ask for help or slow down or admit failure, you fall into a shame spiral that usually involves eating your feelings and stalking exes on social media. Probably once a month or once every two, you reach a point of overwhelm and frustration, and you break down into a crying mess who is certain you're going to die from exhaustion. This lasts for a day or two and then you force yourself to get back up and you start all over again, because you didn't learn a damned thing.

You know how I know all this? Because this is me, too. I told you, I'm not perfect. I'm just speaking from experience here.

I get the need to prove yourself. You either feel the need to prove yourself to your peers, or to your spouse, or to your-own-damn-self that you're still strong and capable and driven. Kids have made you stronger, not a weak butt of some joke. You can still chew iron and spit nails, and everyone can go fuck themselves as you prove that it's not at all unrealistic to do everything and still find the energy to hide in the bathroom just in time for your nervous breakdown to begin. You'll show them. You'll show them all.

Ok, but why? You're a parent, not a demigoddess. You're a human, not a hero. Why do we care so much about proving our worth, especially when it's so wrongly measured in the first place?

"But Arianna," you say, rewinding that Disney commercial for the 90th time, "I'm my *child's* superhero."

My son introduced a hero he made up the other day who propels himself with boogers and tries to pants people. Kids have all of the super-heroism they need residing in their imaginations. They're perfectly happy with real humans who are cool with simply *being* human, instead of pushing themselves to unreasonable breaking points.

What do I mean by this? Simple: Things that we usually give ourselves pats on the back for should remain in the hands of the superheroes. Obviously I'm not talking about making breakfast for your kids even when you're hungover or taking them to a godawful child's birthday party because it makes them happy; that's regular parent stuff that we have to do. I'm talking about stuff like:

Not allowing yourself to get tired

I love naps. If naps were people I'd marry every nap I've ever taken. If naps were old ladies, I would help them across the street and visit them every Sunday. Napping is my favorite hobby, and I am at least upper-level intermediate at it. When my children turn down naps, I'm confused because pooping and sleeping are two of the only unadulterated joys left in my life.

Once kids entered the picture, I stopped getting very many naps. I was still tired, but I wasn't ever allowed to admit that I was. Actually, I was *allowed* to do whatever I wanted, but if I napped, I ran the risk of getting funny looks, or hearing about how people wished *they* had the time for naps. It was almost as if parenthood suddenly meant I wasn't allowed to actually do anything about being tired anymore.

I'm shocked to see that there are still some of us who see tiredness as a weakness. We'll push ourselves until we're getting migraines or muscle tweaks or some other bodily warning that we're working way too hard. We don't take the hint that our minds and bodies try to give us --at least, we don't until it's too late -- and we find this sick sense of pride in it.

"I've just been going so hard that I *crashed* on Saturday." I've heard people crow. "I was just so wrapped up in getting things done that I forgot to sleep."

Why do we treat life as if it's some sort of marathon or Olympic sport with a prize at the end of it? You know what the prize is for all of us? Death. We all die. Then we either get to feed worms or we float on the wind as ashes until we find some place to settle and worsen some poor person's allergies. No one is waiting at the end to congratulate us for all of the times we've sacrificed our health or our comfort. No one is going to applaud you for staying awake for three days straight when you didn't have to. Your dedication isn't being measured by how exhausted and miserable you are.

We do this to each other a lot. We try to one-up one another with stories of how tired we are and how overworked we are, as if that's the real barometer of our dedication. We glare suspiciously at chirpy, happy parents who admit to getting 11 hours of sleep a night. We've decided that parenthood isn't real unless you're constantly fighting your own instincts to slow down and take it easy sometimes, because...that's not what real badasses do or something? I don't know. All I know is, whatever we're telling ourselves, it's a lie. There's nothing badass about putting yourself and your own needs last.

I'm thinking that maybe it's time to set up a new stereotype, one that suggests that it's cool for Mom to be so over it sometimes that she needs counseling or a vacation or just to be left alone for a while. Like, maybe we should start being OK with the fact that we don't always have to max out our to-do list in order to feel "super."

In fact, that brings me to the next thing:

Doing ALL THE THINGS

Good lord, we worship at the almighty shrine of "busy" as a species, don't we? It's our favorite brag. We always talk about how busy we are with a sigh and a slight laugh, like it's actually fun to have days that are packed tight all the goddamned time.

I know that this is a thing, because I fall into this, too. I get off on seeing multiple different colors in my planners for every day of the month. When people mention how they've noticed I'm doing "so many things at once," I actually feel a tiny prick of pride in my chest. That's right: I'm busy. I'm busy, and I'm handling it, and that makes me a total badass.

Except it really doesn't. I've noticed that this message gets lost, especially in motherhood. We're suddenly juggling schedules and projects for multiple people, and so it's imperative that we do these things without asking for help and without making a mistake. After all, motherhood is our "job," right? No one wants to suck at their job. So we look forward to proving to everyone that we have the mental and emotional fortitude to remember lessons, school assignments, doctor's appointments, work deadlines, health goals, and social stuff on our own and with ease. We can't wait to show everyone that we're not the kind of mom who *just sits around*. We're out there *doing stuff*. And we're doing it well. And we're showing that we're strong and capable to the point where we can't wait for our comic book to come out.

Except...I mean...is that really what defines "strong" and "capable?" Are we really stronger because we don't know how to admit when we need someone else, or because we let mistakes define whether or not we're good at being parents? Is that what those words mean? Have you ever really given any thought to that? If you haven't, it's not your fault. The blame actually goes to hustle culture.

Hustle culture is bullshit. Sorry if you don't agree. Actually, no I'm not. I can't help it if you're wrong.

If you aren't familiar with the term, "hustle culture" is a concept that's been bandied about, suggesting that you're a badass or a momboss or a badass momboss or a badboss momass if you're *always* working on something. If you're not working one job, you're working three. If you don't work outside the home, you're busting your ass triple being a stay-at-home-mom. If you aren't busy with kids' lessons and social obligations, you're busy passing out from exhaustion and snapping at everyone out of stress. If you aren't constantly busy, hustle culture suggests, you'd better be *thinking* about being busy, because only people who are always moving and on the edge of a total breakdown actually get anywhere in life. It's all about the hustle. The constant, unending hustle.

Like I said: Bullshit.

"How dare you, Arianna!" You say, giving me the finger. "I make the choices in my life, and I'm choosing to hustle. I'm choosing to do it *all* because I love it."

I don't totally believe you. Not that I think you're a full-on liar, but I definitely don't think you're being honest with yourself. Know why?

Because I bet that, if I was a fly on the wall during 100 of your conversations I'd hear, like, 99 instances wherein you agreed to do what was asked of you immediately, without thinking, and maybe one – if that – wherein you made the choice *not* to do something because you stopped to think and realized you really just didn't want to. I bet that it didn't just occur to you until you read that last sentence that you can actually choose *not* to do things just as readily as you can choose *to* do them. And, in my humble opinion, if you're not exercising both sides of your ability to decide, you're not using it to its full potential. Which means you're also not consciously thinking about how tired you may actually be underneath all that *go, go, go.*

Stress is not an indicator of how good a mother you are. Being bogged down with work and obligations doesn't make you a superhero – it makes you awful at time management. Superheroes don't reschedule things because their adventures have to fit within a small number of pages. Your story spans much longer than that, so how about you put some shit off, set some shit for tomorrow, and allow yourself to rest when you need to rest? Are you seeing a pattern here? Cause I sure am.

Oh, also there's:

Being two (or more) separate people

So you know how no one has ever seen Diana Prince and Wonder Woman in the same place at the same time? You know how that's the whole fun of superheroes, that they have hidden aliases that no one knows about? They're never the same people at once. They're either mild-mannered and they fly under the radar, or they're wearing an alarmingly tight set of pajamas, nearly getting killed trying to make sure everyone else is safe.

You don't have an alter ego; both the mild-mannered every-person and the tough freedom-fighter are parts of you, and you shouldn't ever feel like you have to hide one or the other for fear of being "found out."

You're "Mom" but you're also many parts of whoever you were beforehand. You're the woman who has to wipe up drool and help with homework, but you're also the powerhouse with great ideas and interminable strength you were before you had kids. They didn't separate because you gave birth; if anything, they just built on top of each other to make you one big tower of awesomeness. In fact, you get to be better than a superhero, because you get to do awesome things while being *yourself* every single day. You get to do shit without having to put on a ridiculous leotard and leap from building to building (unless that's what you do, then carry on and pretend this sentence doesn't exist).

So instead of pretending there's a "Mommy" you and a "you" you, just accept the fact that they're all part of the same whole. This way, you won't feel quite as obligated to do the impossible, because you're still pretty in touch with what you can do and what you can't. That is, when you can help it. Which brings me to the next thing that we need to quit feeling contracted to do:

Being Fearless

Yes, you're going to have to get over a *lot* of hang ups. It's part of parenthood; that much is true. You just don't have to get over *everything*, and you don't have to get over everything immediately, or gracefully even.

Take me for example. Remember that Costa Rica saga I told you I'd share? Well, it's time. It's a long one, so I hope you don't have anything you need to be doing. It goes like so:

In 2018, I went to Costa Rica. My husband had an amazing year at work, and they treated all their top salespeople to an all-inclusive trip. We spent a good three months working out and planning and scheming, talking wistfully of the best way to use our time filled with free booze and no kids. I actually dropped some inches off my waist and missed bread a lot. It was a good time to be alive.

The plan, had it all worked out perfectly, was supposed to go like this: we'd leave on a Thursday and return on a Tuesday. During that time, my brother and sister-in-law would stay at our house and drop the kids off at daycare, go to work, and feed our children in the evening. Then, on Saturday or Sunday, my mother-in-law and father-in-law would drive up to take over for the last few days. It took a lot of finagling and profuse thanking, but it was well planned out, and the morning we left, I was excited.

As you've probably already figured, none of that actually happened.

What *did* happen all began while we were on the tarmac at LAX, waiting for the plane to be cleared for takeoff. My husband suddenly gets a message from my brother-in-law:

You daughter has no childcare this morning.

My heart drops into my stomach. As my husband returns the message, I call the daycare. To their credit, they sound apologetic when they tell me that my kid is going to have to go home and stay home, because she'd vomited twice already that morning. I tell them we're on a plane in another state, but that my brother-in-law will be by to pick her up. We hang up, and I start to feel like this might be a situation where hyperventilation is a good idea.

Somehow, I hold it together enough to try to find someone to take over. In this new city that I've only lived in a handful of months, I'm supposed to find someone who I trust to take care of my kid. Not only that, but I have to find a person who doesn't mind being around a pukey toddler. The search continues until we lose all Wi-Fi flying over Mexican airspace, and then I just sit in the sky, worrying about my baby. It's literally the only thing I can think of for the four or so hours it take us to land.

As soon as we get into the hotel, we video call our daughter, only to see that she seems relatively fine, albeit a little quiet. In that same moment, my husband finds out a friend of his can at least watch our daughter the day after. My son is waving and screeching as usual, and

I begin to feel silly. Silly Arianna, shitting herself over a totally nothing occurrence. What will she shit herself over next? What a baby.

All of this was on Thursday.

Friday passes without incident. My husband's friend watches our daughter, I start trying to relax, and even use the harrowing story of my daughter's sickness to break the ice and connect with new people. I make impressions on some of the upper management in my husband's company, because I am goddamned delightful. Things are looking amazing, and I'm finally enjoying myself.

Then comes Saturday.

Saturday morning, for some reason, includes a mandatory business meeting that spouses are "encouraged to attend." I've worked in corporate America long enough to know that this means "bring your spouse or we'll judge you," so I have to go. On the bright side, there's free champagne, so I just sit, double-fisting champagne flutes through the whole three hours, because I am incredibly fucking supportive on top of being goddamned delightful. Even now, I'm not sure what I did to keep from getting bored; maybe I was so bored I blacked out? I don't know. There's a bit of a hole in my memory there.

What I do remember is seeing my husband staring at his phone about five minutes before the end. He looks concerned.

I lean over and whisper: "What's wrong?"

He doesn't look at me. His mouth is almost a straight line. "My debit card was used at a convenience store for like, $80."

"Oh my God."

"Yeah, I'm just gonna cancel it and I guess I'll figure it out when we get home."

The moment those words leave his mouth, my phone buzzes with an email. I read the email twice before tugging on my husband's arm. "It says here my credit card was used at a Taco Bell and a Famous Footwear. Eight dollars and $425."

We stare at each other. In horror movies, this is when the ominous cello music would start to swell. We're the unwitting protagonists, and it's beginning to look like we're about to get chopped up and eaten by cannibals. Metaphorically, of course.

The meeting ends, and everyone stands. My husband's phone rings immediately. He's quiet for a couple of seconds, and then his eyes harden.

"What's wrong?" I ask.

He mouths back "The car was stolen."

Jesus hula-hooping Christ, that's not what I was expecting to hear. My husband told me later that his sister started the phone call with "don't be mad," which is the most counterintuitive thing to say ever. I don't know one person who has stopped being mad because they were told not to be. Instead, people should just be honest from the jump. They should start with "this is going to make you shit yourself and start screaming, so you might as well put on a Depends and get ready." Then at least we all know what we're in for.

At least she tried, I guess. Anyway.

Sister-in-Law advises us that apparently, the friend who watched our daughter the night before parked in front of our garage. Inside the garage is where we always — *always*— park our car. Brother-in-Law, who'd used our car to pick my son up from daycare, couldn't get into the garage to park. So he stopped in our driveway and decided he would come back later to return our car to the garage once the path was clear again. He forgot. This was the only day that our car was ever or has ever been parked in our driveway. It just so happened to also be the one day that two dudes high on meth and looking for trouble decided to stroll through our neighborhood. They tried door handle after door handle until our car popped open. I wasn't there, but I also assume they looked in the center console, found our emergency cards, and figured that it was time to do all the things they'd been wanting to do forever, like buying almost $500 in shoes and messing with total strangers from 1000 miles away. There was no footage; our camera didn't catch a thing. It *did* capture the moment my sister-in-law saw the car was missing, and that was kind of funny, but otherwise it was a shitty situation that we weren't home to deal with.

If you want a good example of cognitive dissonance, imagine you're in the most beautiful tropical paradise you've ever seen. The sun is shining, and the weather is absolutely perfect without humidity. The wind is whispering ever-so-gently through palm trees as they sway lazily against bluer-than-blue skies. It is one of, if not *the*, most beautiful day to be alive, and you're on the phone trying to stay calm as you talk to police and insurance companies about a stolen car. Instead of thinking about cute little drinks with umbrellas in them, you're trying not to think about the fact that your kids' car seats were in the car. You try not to think of what they might be doing to the upholstery. Strangely, you feel a little embarrassed because there was a *lot* of trash in there left over from road snacks.

This is my Saturday, and I'd like to point out that I handle this rather well. I don't do what I want to do, which is demand a plane ticket home and pretend this trip never existed. Instead, I put on a cheerful front and giggle with my husband about how we'll probably have to get a minivan now. We play the "at least" game, listing all the ways things could've been worse. I'm mad, but I'm handling it. I'm still in Costa Rica, and I'm still on vacation, such as it is. It's time to just let go and relax.

Just an aside here --one that doesn't necessarily have to do with being a superhero or parenthood pressures – but the obsession we have with being positive and finding silver linings no matter what is the most fuckety fuck fucked bullshit thing I've ever heard. It's damaging, it's invalidating, and it's unrealistic. We feel pressured to put positive spins on *everything*, lest we become the party buzzkill. You know I've heard people praise children with literal *cancer*, saying: "She's so brave. You know she hasn't complained once?"

WHAT?! CHECK ON HER. She absolutely, 100% should be complaining. Chemo sucks. She's lost her hair. She's sicker than many people will ever be in their lives. She deserves to complain. We're going to praise her for not sharing her negative feelings and making you sad? Fuck you.

If you're sad, be sad. Talk about why you're sad. Quit worrying about whether or not other people will be "brought down" by your sadness. You have a right to be unhappy, and masking that or making light of your problems isn't worth the empty admiration you get for it. Fuck those people. Be sad if you want.

Rant over. Let's talk about what happened to me on Sunday during the Trip from Hell.

We find out first thing Sunday morning that our car was found. That's where the good news ends. Apparently, the two gentlemen who'd stolen our car were quite pissed to find out that we'd canceled the cards, and so they used the car to rob a bar on the northeast end of town. They shoved guns into the poor bartender's face and made off with about $100 and some scratch-off tickets before they tried to escape, driving over spike strips the police had already deployed. Then they lost control of their car —sorry, *our* car — and went careening into four other vehicles, totaling them all.

It's funny, the things you remember. I remember exactly what I was wearing, and exactly which way I was facing when I heard this news. I remember my husband trying to laugh this off, and my own good humor starting to dissipate. I remember taking a couple of deep breaths and telling myself that I didn't want that car back anyway, as I really didn't want to think about what kind of bodily fluids were probably in the seat cracks at that point.

I put the phone down and tell my husband that I'm just glad it's over. Then we leave on our excursion, which is great. We go to the eco-park I mentioned earlier, and except for almost shitting myself with fear while zip lining, things are amazing. All in all, it's an A+ day.

But. We're out of Wi-Fi range all day, and I begin to smell the familiar stink of doom wafting in from the horizon. I feel like Sunday isn't done with me yet.

Spoiler alert: It wasn't.

We get back to the hotel, and the moment Wi-Fi is re-engaged, my husband's phone goes off with a flood of messages. My daughter is back to vomiting, and it looks like my son is about to start, too. Both children are miserable, and this seems to be an ongoing bout that isn't ending any time soon. So at this point, my car has been stolen and crashed in an admittedly-kind-of-cool fashion, and my kids are sick a while away from me, where I can't help.

One thing that I neglected to mention: I can't handle vomiting. I can do any other bodily excretion but puke. When someone around me even starts complaining of a stomachache, my anxiety tops out to the point where I want to run out of the house and not come back until they've finished. And if *I* have to throw up? Forget it. I turn into a pacing, rambling mess who doesn't calm down until the nausea passes. As you'd imagine, having this phobia and having kids makes me real fun to be around during flu season. I'm well aware that this isn't healthy, but it's a problem I have. So deep down, I know that if I had been at home when this all happened, I'd have spent more time pushing my children into the bathroom with a broom and covering my ears so I wouldn't have to hear the retching. I don't actually *want* to help, which adds a level of complication I wasn't prepared for: It fills me with soul-wrenching guilt. Lots of it.

Despite knowing that my mother-in-law is actually the perfect person for this problem because spew doesn't make her…well, want to spew, I feel like I'm failing my kids by not being there to comfort them in whatever small way I can. I'm compelled by this innate need to be there to rub their backs, or at least tell my husband to rub their backs while I try not to look or listen to it. And, on top of this, I know how distressing the act can be. I imagine them going through that fear and that discomfort, and I feel absolutely horrible that I can't do anything for them. I'm scared for them, and I can't shake feeling like I'm wrong for not being there.

I spend the wee hours of Monday morning staring forlornly at my phone. Every time a motion alert goes off on the monitors in my kids' rooms, I check it. I watch them throw up, watch my poor mother-in-law — in different outfits each time from being puked on — take them for baths and change their bedding. My own stomach is in knots, but I feel like I have to do *something*, and watching and crying feels like something. Finally, at about 2 AM, I shut off the notifications on my and my husband's phones and force myself to sleep.

I spend the rest of Monday in a foul mood. I'm telling people about what's going on at home, but there's no mirth. I drink and talk super loudly about how I'm ready to go home. I twitch every time my husband's phone goes off. I'm not fun to be around and I legitimately don't care. Being the drunk curmudgeon at the party is kind of freeing in its own way, but I have to admit it's not as fun as you'd think. Monday ends with me sitting on the floor of our hotel room sobbing, because this is the only real vacation I'm getting for the whole year, and it's turned into a game of Handle Shit at Home, Just From a Different Country.

Tuesday I'm in a fantastic mood, because we get to go home. And even though I spend the next two weeks trying to put shit back to rights, it gets there. That normalcy puts me back in a pretty okay place for a while, and I'm only a little mad when people bring up Costa Rica.

So why am I telling you this, you ask? What's my point? Is this just me trying to make you listen to my bitching?

Ok, rude, but no. My point is this, friend: After that trip, I was petrified to go out of the country ever again. As in, my husband told me his company was paying for Thailand the following year, and my immediate response was "I'm not going." I was maybe 25% kidding. I wanted to stay home with my children, watching them like a hawk and not interacting with people until they went to college and I'd started talking to a puppet I'd made out of my own hair. That's safe. And after last year, I only wanted safe.

I had panic attacks. I had to go to therapy. I had to start taking anxiety medication. All of this was brought on by the fact that I feared from the depths of my soul that things would go badly again. Maybe this time the house would burn down, or my five-year-old would run off to join a biker gang, or my three-year-old would get busted in a dog fighting ring. The possibilities were endless, and I couldn't stop obsessing over each and every one of them.

After thinking about it more than I really wanted to, I realized I needed to do whatever I could to force myself to go on the next trip. I needed to do it to prove to my kids that Mom still does shit even when it might be a little scary sometimes, and I needed to do it to prove to myself that I'm an adult and that I can handle a little fear. Okay, a lot of fear. But I needed to be able to see the world like I've always wanted. I needed to be able to stare things down that seem horrifying in order to see things that are wonderful. I needed to show my kids that a bad time once doesn't mean a bad time always. Also, I heard you can pet elephants in Thailand and I needed to pet a fucking pachyderm.

I did realize, though, that fears aren't always dragons that we have to conquer in order to get through life. In fact, we're taught a little too often that we should be afraid of fear, that we're not free until we escape it fully. There are whole books dedicated to overcoming fears so that you can be the hyper-successful dynamo you always knew you'd be; we know how badly we all want to be unafraid of everything.

My fears, though, were completely understandable considering the circumstances, and trying to simply dismiss them as pesky and irrational wasn't going to help anything. Instead, I had to learn to appreciate them, live with them, and make room for new experiences that *may* eventually put me back to rights. Being afraid *is* pesky, but it isn't always something you can just talk yourself out of, and that's okay. Sometimes, what you need is someone to guide you through it, or to help with as little judgement as possible, to get you started on the path to being stronger. Sometimes, that won't be enough. Sometimes, those fears of yours are totally and completely understandable and reasonable, and you won't be able to do anything with them besides respect them. No matter the situation, the best thing to do is to accept your limitations in that moment, and to do what you can. Be happy with what you're able to do, and let the new stuff come to you as you're ready.

You are going to be afraid, and sometimes, there won't be a whole lot you can do about it.

This is true especially once you have children, because as they get older you lose control over everything they do. This would be fine if kids always used caution and common sense, but they don't, so you're going to have to worry about them making bad decisions until you're almost dead. You will be afraid for them. You will be afraid to allow them to do things. You will be afraid to allow *yourself* to do things, because you have someone counting on you and your death would be horribly inconvenient. Sometimes, you will be victorious, and sometimes you won't be. What you have to realize is this: Being fearless isn't what makes you great. Overcoming all of your fears isn't what makes you great. It's owning those fears and learning to function despite them that makes all the difference.

Also, your fears sometimes keep you alive. So I mean…Wonder Woman can afford to be fearless; you can't.

For the record, I did the therapy. And I took the meds. And I got on the plane to Thailand, and I had a wonderful time. I still have anxiety, though, and I'm still not completely over the vomiting thing. Despite those very human idiosyncrasies, I'm still parenting children who are decent people the majority of the time. I didn't need a Lasso of Truth to do that.

Though one of those *would* be pretty cool.

Last but not least, we need to quit expecting ourselves to do this:

Win every battle, all the time

To be completely fair, this isn't just a mom thing. This is a people thing, and the countless books and podcasts and seminars prove it. We all want to be "winners," whatever that means, and so we're obsessed with being the last one standing for everything. A lot of the self-help novels we read will be all about how to kick ass and take names and wind up the victor by thinking really hard about what you want or "just going for it."

I want to make it clear here that I agree, to a point. I totally understand why this outlook motivates people, and I've partaken quite a few times myself. Knowing that you have control of everything that happens to you, knowing that you have it in you to succeed if you try hard enough, is empowering. Then, you don't have to believe that the universe is just taking shit from you because it feels like it.

You didn't get that promotion because you didn't try hard enough.

You never became a famous musician because you weren't ballsy enough.

Your kid's speech isn't as good as other kids their age because you just haven't put in enough time or effort to fix it. It's all on you to shape your destiny, and you'll wind up only where you want to wind up, and you'll only ever get what you put in. You *could* have it, you just don't because you needed to put in more *effort*.

Maybe I'm just lazy, but doesn't that sound fucking *exhausting?* Why does every little thing that happens – or doesn't happen – have to be on you? Why do you have to be the absolute controller of your destiny, especially when you can't even fully control someone who's half your size? What about that is appealing?

Being in control is fun and all, but we're not 100% in control of everything that happens to us. Unless you live in a bubble, you're part of a macrocosm filled to the brim with outside influences. There are other people out there with free will and their own set of values. There are right and wrong places to be at right and wrong times. The grace of others is a thing. Luck is a thing.

No one really likes hearing about luck because it sounds fake, and it removes power. How are you supposed to feel like you're strong and empowered if the universe is responsible for positives and negatives in your life? What am I trying to do? Depress you? Who the hell thought it would be a good idea for you to buy this book anyway? Time to write a complaint email.

I'm not saying that you have no control over anything; I *am* saying that you're not omniscient. You don't control what talents you were born with or how others will feel about you on sight. You can work your fingers to the bone on a project and that project can just fail. It can have nothing to do with anything you did, and have everything to do with components just not working together very well. You can be nicer than is humanly possible to someone, only to have them mistreat you anyway. That isn't because you said or did anything wrong; it's because sometimes, people are just terrible. Walking away from any of that with an attitude of failure, as if you could have controlled things that you couldn't, is just asking to swim in unnecessary guilt until you finally drown.

For example, when I was pregnant with my son, all of the birth classes told me about the magic that would be breastfeeding. I was told about the bonding with the baby, the sweet music that would play from nowhere, and the little woodland creatures that would gather at my feet. I was never told that I wouldn't be able to make enough for my son, or that, despite eating countless lactation cookies, drinking special teas, guzzling water, and making voodoo dolls, there might just be a chance that I wouldn't be a very good milk producer. I didn't know any better, so I spent my time thinking that I wasn't trying hard enough. It took me a while to understand that this was a battle that had other factors to it, and I wish someone had told me about it.

I also see constant reminders in my battles with my own mental health. I don't think I can stress enough how hard it is when you can't control your *own goddamned brain*. It's one thing having an asshole friend who points out all of your fuck ups with glee. You can just drown that person out, or choose not to hang out with them anymore. When your constant fears and judgements and doubts are coming from within, however, what are you supposed to do? Your own brain is already telling you how shitty you are, so that's been done. You can't kick yourself out of your own head. So you're just…sort of stuck together.

Medications have shitty side effects. No medication means you're sucking down CBD and melatonin and using weighted blankets and going on walks, and sometimes, you're still overwhelmed and scared and thinking you might puke. I've had days where I've fought with my brain with all I had, and I've still wound up curled up in the fetal position, sobbing at the end of the day because I'm certain I'm going to die. I've spent hours fighting valiantly and still lost. In those moments, all you can do is tell yourself that if you make it another 12 hours/30 minutes/whatever, it'll get better and you'll feel normal-ish again. It all becomes about little moments where you win, and accepting the moments you don't.

By the way, if you're someone like me, take care of yourself and give yourself grace. I'm not gonna tell you how to live your life, but don't forget that you're not on your own. If you can, accept help from professionals. I promise you there's no shame in it. And even if you feel a little shame, when you're feeling like yourself again, you won't give a shit. Just putting that out there.

Anyway.

I feel like there are people out there who find real strength in thinking of themselves as a super-powered strongwoman. I want to make it clear that if you find true motivation in being larger-than-life and powerful-as-a-raging-fire-mysterious-as-the-dark-side-of-the-moon, go for it. All that I ask is that you really, *really* pay attention to how you feel when trying to match up to that ideal. More importantly, how do you feel when you *don't* match up? Do you fly off into the sunset ready to fight again? Or do you constantly feel like the weight of the world is crushing you and catch yourself wishing you had a villain's origin story instead?

If you really must be a superhero, try to redefine what that means to you. Make it something you can attain; not something a traditional superhero can attain, not something someone else can attain, but something *you* can take for your own. Then do what you can to achieve that. When you fall, try to bounce back. When you don't feel like you *can* bounce back, lick your wounds and allow yourself some grace. The sooner you're able to accept that view, the sooner you're able to do great things that build you up in a way you, particularly, need. Your way may not net you any book or movie deals, but I'm more than certain that you'll find many people – the *right* people – who are interested in your origin story.

Fuck, that was corny. But if it helped you, then I have no regrets.

What I'm saying here is that you shouldn't feel like you're only extraordinary if you "win." You're not extraordinary only when you're getting your kids to eat their veggies or go to bed on time. Winning doesn't make you worthy of note; finding it within yourself to recover after a big loss, and to fight again tomorrow is what makes you worthy. And doing it because your annoying-ass kids need you to is what makes you Mom. Not Wonder Woman, not a "Super Mom."

Just Mom.

That, in itself, is powerful enough.

Epilogue

So I guess that's it. Hopefully, something I've learned has helped you out; I know that we tend to feel often like no one gives us advice that makes sense for us. If I've failed at giving helpful advice, at least I've given you ample time to shit with the door closed for a bit. If I haven't done that then…I don't know. Use this to correct the wobbly tables in your house. I help however I can.

If you don't take anything else from all of the random musings in this book, I want you to take this: No one gets to dictate your story but you. As trite as that might sound, you are only a quitter or a success or an evil genius if you decide you are. Contrary to popular belief, your children didn't remove your ability to choose your story – they just added a chapter or two. You define yourself, you define your happiness (and unhappiness), and you define your past, present, and future. Use that to make sure that the definition is one that you're happy with, and then don't let anyone – not your family, not your friends, and not some jerk lady writing a book in her robe at 6:30 in the morning – tell you whether or not that definition should change.

I know that's easier said than done, especially in our digital age when everyone thinks their opinion carries weight just because. What you also have to remember is, you're a mom. You know how to tune things out. If you didn't, you'd have to hear "Mom. Mom. Mom" 6,459,952 times and you'd probably wind up leaving your kid outside a fire station somewhere.

So I mean…use that skill, that amazing mom ability, to tune out the extra noise. Only tune in when it's important or life-changing, and let the rest of them figure out what to do with their impressions of you.

Just…y'know…don't be a dick about it. The whole point here is that we're flawed, and that means we don't know half as much as we think we do. So don't be afraid to learn from others, even if they're people you can't half stand.

Accept that you're fallible, allow in some advice once in a while, but use your heart and your gut and your mind (you know, that thing they like to say you lost when you had kids?) to help you figure out what applies and what doesn't. Blanket approaches help no one, least of all your family.

We need each other, whether we like it or not. Be nice to one another, even if the other person is someone you're not particularly interested in hanging out with. You don't have to invite them over to your house, but you can help when they're struggling.

And be nice to *you*. Make yourself more of a priority sometimes. Allow yourself to fuck up. Allow yourself to fuck up big, sometimes multiple times in a row. Don't beat yourself up over past messes and just allow yourself to clean up what you see in front of you right now. Remind yourself that your missteps don't always count for more just because you're Mom. Allow yourself to remember that you've gained sudden charge of what's basically a turkey-sized Martian with the survival instinct of a lemming, and you were never given a manual on how to work it. Sure, there are tons of books out there about Martian turkey-lemmings, but they're a crap shoot, because they're not about *your particular* Martian turkey-lemming. So you're learning. You're always learning, and learning calls for making mistakes sometimes.

You've got this. It's not always going to feel like you've got this, but you do. People have been living and feeling and succeeding without instruction manuals for millions of years, and many of them are much dumber than you are.

So close this book and start doing whatever you need to do remind yourself of the powerhouse, the presence, and the *person* that you are.

Or don't. I'm not your mom.

ACKNOWLEDGEMENTS

Thank you a million times to these people:

My husband, Mark, for having no idea what I'm babbling about, but being 100% supportive regardless.

My two babies for giving me endless entertainment, and a constant wellspring of content. And for brightening my world and making me a mother, I guess.

Sarah M., Sam Lewis, Mom, and Maren: Thank you for looking through this madness and giving me your honest opinions. I don't know where this thing would be without you.

Sarah M. again, Jennifer, Claire, Sam, Pam, Rachel, Lacey, and Amie for showing me what good friends do.

Sam Lewis and Mark Heaps for their support and constant mentoring.

Pam for brilliant cover design advice.

Cobalt PDX Studios for guidance and workspace.

My dad, Fidel, for giving me half of my sense of humor, and half my genes.

Dee, Other Sarah, Rhyming Sarah, Jessica, Gretel, Kelly, Patty, Melissa, Liz, Mary, Elin, Roy, Crockett, Dean, Chad, Ash, Jonesy, Josh, Kane, Michelle, Abbey, Kenzie, and Carly for being some of the best friends and sounding boards I could possibly have without meeting you face to face.

You, for reading this, and for doing everything to be the best parent you can. Go, you rockstar, you.

WORKS CITED

Haaland, M. "Nearly Half of Women have Been Affected by Hormonal Imbalance." *The New York Post* 22 Feb. 2019.

Hall, Jeffrey A. "How Many Hours Does it Take to Make a Friend?" *Journal of Social and Personal Relationships* (2018): 1278-1296.

Knapton, S. "Parenthood Leaves Half of Mothers and Fathers Feeling Lonely." *The Telegraph* Nov. 2017.
Peanut. *Inside the Secret Sex Lives of Millennial Moms.* Aug. 2018. <https://www.peanut-app.io/millennialmomsurvey>.

S. Fischman, E. Rankin, K. Soeken, E. Lenz. "Changes in Sexual Relationships in Postpartum Couples." *Principles and Practice* (1986): 58-63.

Warnick, Melody. *Why You're Miserable After a Move.* 13 Jul 2016. <https://www.psychologytoday.com/us/blog/is-where-you-blong/201607/why-youre-miserable-after-move>.

Wiebke Bleidorn, et. al. "Stability and Change in Self-Esteem During the Transition to Parenthood." *Social Psychological and Personality Science* (2016).

ABOUT THE AUTHOR

ARIANNA BRADFORD is the lead editor and writer at the NYAM Project, and host of the podcast of the same name. She was chosen as one of Huffington Post's Funniest Twitter Parents of 2019, and has been seen on the likes of Scary Mommy, Romper, and The Chive. She lives in Oregon with her husband and two kids.

To keep up with and/or contact the NYAM Project, visit www.wearenyam.com.

To reach out to Arianna directly, visit www.theariannabradford.com

Manufactured by Amazon.ca
Bolton, ON

13494645R00094